HAS SIN CHANGED?

HAS SIN CHANGED?

Seán Fagan, S.M.

Michael Glazier, Inc.
Wilmington, Delaware

First Published in 1977 by Michael Glazier, Inc.,
1210A King Street, Wilmington, Delaware 19801

Copyright © 1977 by Seán Fagan, S.M.

International Standard Book Number: 0-89453-086-0

Library of Congress Card Catalog Number: 77-91879

Typographical Designer - Alvin Schultzberg

Typography - Robert Zerbe

ACKNOWLEDGEMENTS

The author and publisher wish to thank the American Bible Society, New York, and William Collins & Co., Ltd., London, for permission to quote from the *Good News Bible*; and are grateful to Costello Publishing Company, New York, and Dominican Publications, Dublin, for permission to quote from *Vatican II: The Conciliar and Post-Conciliar Documents*, translated by Austin Flannery, O.P.

TABLE OF CONTENTS

1

WHAT HAPPENED TO SIN?

Sin is not a fashionable word nor a popular subject in today's world. For non-religious people it is simply irrelevant, a carry-over from a bygone age, now devoid of meaning. Even in religious circles it has not the common currency it once had. Among Christians its meaning has become confused to such an extent that preachers and teachers tend to soft-pedal it. In the flood of religious writing that followed the Second Vatican Council, it received only minor attention. Just a few years ago, its near-disappearance provoked Dr. Karl Menninger to write a book with a question for its title: *Whatever Became of Sin?* As one of the most eminent psychoanalysts of our time, he acknowledged the wide variety of factors that can lessen human freedom, and in describing the mess that people make of their lives and the evil they can cause in the world, he made full allowance for the influence of heredity, environment, instinctual drives and subconscious motivation. But he insisted that there is still such a thing as moral responsibility. To emphasize this conviction he pleaded for a revival of the word 'sin' and suggested that the world would be a healthier place if we showed more concern for repentance and conversion. As a psychiatrist he explained that it does little good to repent a symptom, but it may do great harm not to repent a sin. He called on clergymen to exercise their spiritual leadership, to preach, to prophesy, to cry out. How? Preach! Tell it like it is! Say it from the pulpit, cry it from the housetops! Sin! Sin! In calling for a revival of the moribund word 'sin', Menninger asked the clergy to reassert their moral leadership, to study sin, identify it, define it,

1

warn people about it, and promote measures to combat and rectify it.

This is indeed the mission of priest, prophet and spiritual leader. There are plenty of biblical precedents for it. The Old Testament prophets continually denounced the misdeeds of the Jewish people as sins. John the Baptist urged his hearers to be converted from their sins. Jesus himself preached repentance, conversion, and told his followers that his body would be broken and his blood poured out for the forgiveness of sins. Sin is a fundamental concept in Christian faith. In fact, we cannot really be Christians unless we are conscious of our sinfulness and recognize our need of Jesus Christ.

Is sin changing?

But sin has had a bad press in recent times. It is no exaggeration to say that there has been a wide-spread loss of the sense of sin, not only in the world at large, but even within the Christian churches. A variety of reasons can be suggested for this. Among church-going people, it may be a reaction against over-emphasis on sin in the past, both in its hell-fire punishment aspect and in the detailed labelling that attached a degree of sinfulness to even the simplest of human activities. Benjamin Rush, the first American psychiatrist, dashed off an open letter to clergy-men of all faiths on the subject of American morality in 1788, in which he condemned as sins 'smoking, drinking, the popular election of judges, the country fair (a temptation to extravagance, gaming, drunkenness and uncleanness), horse racing, cock fighting, dining at men's clubs, and enjoying oneself on the sabbath by swimming, sliding, and skating'. It is easy to smile at such a list and murmur condescendingly about the Puritan ethic. But Catholics have no grounds for complacency. Until a short time ago it was considered a venial sin for a priest to celebrate Mass without a biretta; it could be mortal if it were done out of contempt. Many people still think that to miss one Sunday Mass deliberately without sufficient reason means hell for all eternity. Though their number is diminishing, there are still people who feel that they need confession before communion if they have a fleeting sexual thought during a television program. Today's common sense rejects such attitudes, but the rejection is often accompanied by an impatience with any talk of sin, and so the real meaning of sin is weakened or lost.

The worldwide decline in respect for authority is another factor. Sin has traditionally been preached as disobedience to God's law as expressed in the bible, church teaching and the commands of lawful authorities. But people are nowadays more alert to the abuses and exaggerations of authority, and find it difficult to see any convincing link between obedience to rules and fidelity to God. This too may be a healthy enough reaction, rejecting the notion of God as primarily legislator and taskmaster, but it can blunt our sensitivity to God's call and blind us to the possibility of sinful refusals.

A new, but not always correct, understanding of conscience may also lessen the sense of sin. Reacting against the blind obedience sometimes preached in the past, many people now confuse personal conscience with doing as they please, without any reference to guidance from authority. 'What is right' very easily becomes 'what I like', and since there is no strong urge in human nature to do what one dislikes, the lines between right and wrong become blurred, moral conflict disappears, and with it the whole notion of sin.

A more general reason for the weakening of the notion of sin is the lessening of the sense of God in today's world. Western society is becoming more and more secularized, with little direct reference to God, so the faults of men are seldom understood as religious realities, as sins. Affluence is a factor here, insofar as riches often bring a sense of independence and self-sufficiency, with little room for God. Jesus himself warned us about this: 'How hard it will be for rich people to enter the kingdom of heaven' (Mt 10:23).

Freedom and responsibility

In the area of freedom and responsibility, the discoveries of psychology about subconscious motivation and the influence of heredity and environment tend to lessen people's sense of guilt and consequently their admission of sin. It is frequently believed that because a motive for an action can be identified, that the action was not fully free, and so the evils in the world can be attributed to outside forces and circumstances beyond our control. It is too easily forgotten that no human action can be without a motive, that our motives are freely chosen, notwithstanding outside influences, and they are often sinfully selfish, without regard for our true good or for the needs of others.

Paradoxically, a somewhat similar form of escapism may be our greater sensitivity nowadays to collective responsibility for sinful situations and structures, for social evils like discrimination, racism, economic exploitation on national and international levels. We can become so righteously indignant about these social injustices not of our making that we forget the personal sins in our own lives. The enormity of some of these unjust structures and our helplessness in the face of them make our personal misdeeds seem trivial by comparison.

Psychologists have discovered a great deal in recent decades about neurotic guilt and the influence of what Freud called the 'super ego'. The general acceptance of these findings by the public at large has tended to weaken the sense of sin, since sin is usually associated with guilt. But writers of popular psychology often fail to distinguish between the irrational guilt feelings produced by infantile conscience and the real guilt acknowledged by a morally mature person who has acted against his conscience. Psychiatrists and counsellors sometimes undermine a person's morale and sense of personhood by telling him that he was not responsible for his actions, instead of helping him to accept his responsibility and real moral guilt. There is a sure-fire remedy for the pain of real guilt: acknowledgment, repentance, atonement. To treat it as neurotic, in those cases in which it is clearly not such, is to ask for trouble. A rehabilitation of the word 'sin' and a greater understanding of how to cope with it through repentance and forgiveness would be more helpful to many people than the guesswork and groping of some psychiatrists.

An over-optimistic view of evolution and human progress can also blunt the concept of sin. It is possible to contrast today's moral sensitivity to human rights with the barbarism and cruelty of former times, but it would be a mistake to conclude that mankind is therefore less sinful. Our greater awareness of certain moral values and our deeper insight into the dignity of man do not mean that we are morally better than our grandparents. The developments of technology that have made life more comfortable and offer us possibilities for a new humanism, have also

opened new roads to unprecedented forms of in-
humanity. The old are often lonelier today than in
most times in the past, people are less capable of
coping with the problem of death in today's society,
and the living conditions in modern cities have not
produced greater friendliness or neighborliness. We
can feel self-righteous in condemning apartheid
abroad, but what happens to our convictions when
we are in a position to do something about racial discrimination in our own neighborhood or in our
business? The torture and oppression practiced by
so many governments throughout the world should be
a warning against a too easy optimism. Sin is still a
reality in our world, and the world might be a healthier place if it were more sincerely and realistically
admitted.

The 'sin-grid'

Catholics have been affected by many of these factors,
but there were elements in our own religious tradition to weaken or distort the notion of sin. Our experience of the sacrament of penance was not always
helpful, and it left many with a very inadequate
notion of sin. They were frequently provided with
what has been called the 'sin-grid', a precise set of
categories of sin for use in the examination of conscience in preparation for confession. Anything which
did not easily fit into this grid might be considered
wrong, but was not always seen as sinful. Sins were
clearly divided into original and actual, mortal and
venial, formal and material. Actual sin was any
thought, word, or deed contrary to the law of God.
It was serious when the matter was grave and the sin
was committed with full knowledge and full consent.
If the matter was not grave in itself, or if the sinner
was ignorant of its gravity, or did not fully consent

to it, the sin was less serious, i.e., venial. Serious sin was mortal, involving the loss of sanctifying grace, which is the divine life in the soul. A sinner dying in this state would go to hell for all eternity. The infinite punishment for a finite act was thought necessary since an offense is measured by the dignity of the person offended. Since God is infinite, the offense was infinite, and so the punishment would be infinite or eternal. This picture was clear and simple; all one needed to know was what constituted grave matter (hence the sin-grid), and the main burden of conscience was to decide on the degree of knowledge or consent.

Large numbers of Catholics lived happy and holy lives with this simple understanding, and there may be some for whom it is still meaningful, or at least not too harmful. But growing numbers are dissatisfied with such an over-simplified picture. It does not speak to their condition, and it raises too many questions for which they have not been given convincing answers. There is a reaction against a legalistic, formalistic, juridic notion of sin as a thing, a breaking of an external law, a disruption of order and stability. There is a greater awareness of man's personal responsibility, a realization that the established order itself, whether in church or state, may be an obstacle to full human development, and so not in accordance with God's will. The dissatisfaction with the older presentation is not always clearly defined or understood, but there is real need for a new understanding of sin. Such a new understanding has indeed developed over the past few years. There is no question of a 'new theology' to do away with sin or encourage the so-called 'permissiveness' of modern society. There is continuity between the old and the new, though a considerable shift of emphasis has taken place, and in many ways the whole question is seen

in a new light. Sin is as much a reality as ever, and
is taken quite seriously by the new theology. In a
sense, the new understanding makes far more demands than the old.

It could be objected that what is needed for the
renewal of the Church is a positive theology of love
rather than a negative theology of sin. This is certainly true, but there is room for a book which will
meet people where they are, which will take what
understanding they already have, and help them to see
where it needs to be corrected and developed. A book
on sin need not be a negative treatment. The good
news of the gospel is that God loves us with an everlasting love, and that this love became incarnate in
Jesus through whom we have the forgiveness of sins.
We cannot repent and be converted unless we take sin
seriously. But a defective notion of sin can produce
distorted ideas of God, the Church, conscience, law,
sacraments (particularly penance), and Christian
morality itself. It may be helpful, therefore, to take
a critical look at those aspects of the common understanding of sin which need correcting and development. A new presentation will not be helpful to people
who are still under the influence of inadequate notions
from the past. To identify and admit that influence
can in itself be a liberating experience.

Problems from the past

The old 'sin-grid' focused attention on measurement,
both of the matter of the sin and of the degree of
responsibility and guilt. This needs re-examination
today. Are the old categories sufficient? They emphasized law, which was always clearly defined,
and therefore easily measured. But with the multiplication of Church laws, people felt that where there
was no clearcut law, there was no moral obligation.

Besides, many came to believe that things were wrong because they were forbidden instead of seeing that they were forbidden because they were wrong. This is hardly moral maturity. Among the commandments, the two relating to sex were singled out for such disproportionately special treatment that many people today automatically think of sex when the word 'sin' is mentioned. If sin is feared, it is often because of the punishment attached to it, but the traditional notions of purgatory and hell are un-convincing to many modern Catholics, so their sense of sin is affected. Not only can parents no longer instil the fear of God into their children by invoking the threat of hell-fire, but they are at a loss when it comes to explaining and handing on the moral principles they themselves were brought up on. They feel par-ticularly helpless in trying to form the consciences of their children, because they themselves were seldom encouraged to explore the full meaning of conscience or to use it in a really personal way. The teaching Church, as a loving mother concerned for the safety of her children, at times developed an over-protective attitude amounting to a nervous distrust of the presence of the Holy Spirit in the faithful. A narrow view of the 'teaching Church' restricted it to the government in the Church, and it was forgotten that the whole Church is both a teaching Church and a learning Church. Because of an individualistic notion of sin, the sacrament of penance became, for many people, a private guilt-shedding process with little reference to the Church itself as a community of reconciliation. Preoccupation with law and meas-urement, coupled with this individualistic notion of sin, left Catholics less conscious of collective respon-sibility and the general sinfulness of the community itself. Likewise, individual sinful actions were often assessed in isolation from the overall pattern of life.

Bits of behavior were often given moral labels in terms of their physical component, without reference to the full human meaning of the action.

Change in the Church

While these various factors have left many Catholics with an inadequate or even distorted notion of sin, it is also true that the confusion they experience is part of the general upheaval in the Church since the Second Vatican Council. Changes were not limited to dogmatic theology, liturgy or ecclesiastical organization, but affected some of the basic principles of Christian morality. The interpretation of the bible, the extent of the Church's teaching authority, and modern insights about the nature of man, all gave rise to new questions in the area of morals. The old black and white answers were no longer convincing, the lines became blurred, and soon people were confused as to what could be labelled sin, or indeed what sin really meant.

Since a defective notion of sin can result in distortions in so many other areas of Christian belief, the following chapters will treat of sin in relation to law, measurement, sex, guilt, punishment, conscience, forgiveness, teaching and preaching, and conclude with a summary of what Christian morality is all about. It could be objected that this is an inversion of the logical procedure, that one should begin with the positive call of God, the fullness of Christian life, and see sin as failure and refusal. It is true that it is more attractive, consoling and challenging to be presented with the ideal before discussing the failure. But it can also be helpful to begin where people are, and many people already have a notion of sin which can be an obstacle to their understanding of the ideal. For example, to judge by the almost neurotic repetition of sins from their past life confessed in their weekly or monthly confession, one wonders if some people *really* believe in God's forgiveness. Even at the risk of seeming to paint a caricature, it may be a service to such people to bring out into the open and face explicitly whatever it is that distorts their notion of sin. It is not a question of the private aberrations of a few immature or neurotic people. All the factors in question are elements in the experience of the Church itself down through the centuries. In describing and analyzing them, there is no intention to criticize simply for the sake of criticism or to make fun of previous generations of Christians. It must be recognized that any new understanding of the Christian message must grow out of, and be in continuity with, the past. But it is a false loyalty to the Church to pretend that it was always perfect, that it could never be short-sighted or one-sided in its understanding and practice. There is no need for us to disown our past; without it we cannot fully understand the present. However, there is no question of merely highlighting the negative elements. We need to rediscover the valid insights from the Church's long experience and develop them in the light of today's needs.

Rehabilitate sin

What is needed is a rehabilitation of the word 'sin', not for its own sake, but in a way that will re-focus and re-vitalize our understanding of Christian morality, help us to accept responsibility for our wrongdoing, and enable us to appreciate the incredible, liberating and re-creating gift we have been given in God's forgiveness. To speak of sin and to reflect on our own sinfulness is not necessarily an exercise in introversion, a pessimistic navel-gazing. On the contrary, it can be a very healthy and profoundly Christian experience. We cannot be Christian unless we feel a real need for Christ, and it is our sinfulness that brings this home to us. The English mystic, Julian of Norwich, was not ashamed to write: 'We need to fall, and we need to realize this. If we never fell, we should never know how weak and wretched we are in ourselves; nor should we ever appreciate the astonishing love of our Maker . . . We sin grievously, yet despite all this it makes no difference at all to his love, and we are no less precious in his sight. By the simple fact that we fall, we shall gain a deep knowledge of what God's love means . . . It is a good thing to know this'. Indeed, it is a very good thing. It makes all the difference between simply knowing *about* God and actually *knowing* God. St. Paul assures us that 'all things work towards good for those who love God'. Commenting on this, St. Augustine added: 'Yes even sin', and he knew what he was talking about.

2

WHAT DOES THE BIBLE SAY?

However weak the sense of sin may be in the world, or whatever the distorted notions of it to be found among Christians, one thing is clear. Evil or wrong-doing is described as sin only when it is understood as directed against God. This is a notion that comes from the bible, where it is a basic concept in both old and new testaments. Before considering the areas of inadequacy or confusion in the modern understanding of sin, therefore, it will be necessary to see what the bible has to say about it. But we must be careful how we interpret the bible. It is a misleading over-simplification to think of the bible as God's revelation dictated to the sacred writers. It is more correctly understood as the written account of the religious experience of the people of God in the old testament and of the Christian communities in the new testament. These writings are inspired in the sense that not only the experience, but the understanding and re-cording of it were under the influence of the Holy Spirit. That experience was primarily of the special relationship of intimacy to which they believed God had called and introduced them.

God's love

It involved a world-view that saw the whole of crea-tion, their political history and their personal lives as a working out of that relationship. For them, God was the infinitely-loving, ever-faithful Father who never went back on his word, who allowed them to renew the covenant he had made with them over and over again, in spite of their repeated infidelities. Down

through the centuries they had gone 'whoring after
false gods'. The old testament is the record of their
sins, their missing the mark, their continual failure
to live up to what God wanted them to be. But it is also
the story of God's love, of his initiative in choosing
them, and of his loving-kindness in continually caring
for them, in spite of their failures. Sin is the foil which
manifests God's incredible goodness, his never-
ending forgiveness.

Their experience of God reached its peak in their
encounter with his incarnate son Jesus, and it is significant that his very name, as explained by Matthew,
refers to the forgiveness of sins: 'you shall call his
name Jesus, because he will save his people from their
sins' (1:21). He began his mission by a call to repentance: 'be converted from your sins'. He spent much
of his time with sinners and outcasts, and just before
his death he summed up his mission in the sublime
words: 'This is my blood which seals God's covenant,
my blood poured out for many for the forgiveness
of sins' (Mt 26:28). The good news preached by the
early church was not simply that Jesus had risen from
the dead, but that in his death and resurrection he
had overcome sin, that in him we have the forgiveness
of our sins. We ask now: what does the bible tell us
about the nature of sin that it is such a fundamental
concept?

God and sin

There is no special word in Hebrew for the theological
notion of sin, but the old testament uses different
words to describe what the Jewish people understood
by sin. The most common is the verb meaning 'to miss
the mark', not simply a mistake in judgment, but a
failure to reach a goal, and this could also be a non-
action, an omission. Other words used were iniquity,

guilt, rebellion, disorder, abomination, lie, folly. From the contexts in which these words occur it is clear that sin was not simply the transgression of a law, but caused a break in the relationship between God and his people. Israel understood this relationship as a covenant, alliance or pact of love, initiated by God himself. Because of this special choice of God, they were his people and were expected to act as the people of God. The laws they devised for their conduct and for the ordering of their society, whether discovered by their own experience or borrowed from the surrounding peoples, were understood as the law of God, coming from God himself. Failure to observe them meant to miss the mark of God's love. It meant to bring about iniquity, a deviation from how things ought to be, and this meant guilt, the distortion produced by sin. Guilt was thought of as a burden too heavy to bear, a rust that eats into a person's soul and remains engraved on the sinner's heart. The description of sin as rebellion is not to be understood in terms of today's political relationships. In the ancient world the relationship between sovereign and servant was one of beneficence, so rebellion was ingratitude and personal insult, much like the rebellion of a child against the goodness of its parents. When sin is described as folly, this is not meant to excuse the sinner with a 'fool's pardon'. The word foolishness is used not to imply diminished responsibility, but to indicate that the sinner becomes foolish by his sin.

But the basic notion of sin throughout the old testament is that of a break in the relationship between God and man. The relationship in question is not primarily between creator and creature, but that between the divine and human partners in a personal union, a mutual relationship of belonging. Israel actually experienced the ever-present love of God through the long years of its history, and in that sense *knew* God, as a wife knows her husband and is known by him. In the regular ceremonies for the renewal of the covenant, the people were sprinkled with the blood of the animal offered to God, to signify a kind of blood-relationship between God and his people, to emphasize that they were his family. But sin separates them from him. The prophet thundered: 'It is your sins that separate you from God when you try to worship him. You are guilty of lying, violence, and murder' (Isaiah 59:2-3). Hosea, Jeremiah and Ezekiel describe the people's sins as marital infidelity, disobedience, pride. Though no action of the creature can really hurt the creator, Jeremiah speaks in God's name with all the sorrow and heartbreak of a deserted husband: "My people, why do you turn away from me without ever turning back? You cling to your idols and refuse to return to me. I listened carefully, but you did not speak the truth. Not one of you has been sorry for his wickedness; not one of you has asked 'What have I done wrong?' Everyone keeps on going his own way, like a horse rushing into battle. Even storks know when it is time to return; doves, swallows, and thrushes know when it is time to migrate. But, my people, you do not know the laws by which I rule you. How can you say that you are wise, and that you know my laws? Look, the laws have been changed by dishonest scribes. Your wise men are put to shame; they are confused and trapped. They have rejected my words; what wisdom have they got now?' (Jer. 8:5-9).

The new testament

This is the background which the new testament writers took for granted. They used the classical Greek noun *hamartia* and the verb *hamartanein* for sin, but turned them into theological terms by giving them a meaning not found in profane sources. To the

old testament understanding they added new elements: that sin is not only an individual act, but also
a state or condition, that it is a power at work in the
world, but it is finally overcome by Jesus. Matthew,
Mark and Luke have little to say abut sin, but it is
significant that what they do have is usually in reference to forgiveness. They present Jesus as the friend
of sinners, embodying by his patience, delicacy and
tact, the mercy of God. In these gospels, it is made
clear that ritual impurity is not a sin, that sins come
from the heart and they alone defile a man (Mt 15:18-
19). Sin is compared to the wandering of a son from his
father's house (Lk 15:18), but he need only ask for
forgiveness and he is immediately received back.

In the writings of John, sin is described as lawless-
ness, unrighteousness. He who sins is from the devil
and is the slave of sin. Sin is the lust of the flesh, the
lust of the eyes, and the pride of life. The sinner loves
darkness rather than the light. More often than not,
John uses the word sin to describe a state rather than
a single act.

The Greek word for sin occurs sixty times in the
letters of Paul, and it is he who has the fullest theology
of sin in the new testament. For him, sin is universal,
something in which every human being is involved.
It is first and foremost a state or condition of human
nature from which sinful acts come. It is a power
which has man in its grip. Man is 'under sin' in the
same way that a child is said to be under its parents,
or an army under its commander. Sin 'lords it over us'
like a despot. Sin 'takes us captive' as prisoners are
taken in war. It is not merely an external power, but
gets right inside us, into our every fibre, so that we
become the 'slaves of sin'. But Paul also affirms our
freedom in the face of sin. We can resist and overcome
sin by Christ dwelling in our hearts, by his spirit
taking possession of us (Rom 8:1-17).

The new testament speaks of the consequences of sin. Sin results in a hardening of the heart, a dulling of the moral sense, so that there is less and less reluctance to sin, and thus sin begets sin. It also results in 'death'. According to Paul it was sin that brought death, both physical and spiritual, into the world. Finally, it brings eternal damnation. In Christ's picture of the last judgment, the wicked are sent out of God's sight: 'Depart from me, you condemned'. Jesus himself speaks of the 'unquenchable fire' of Gehenna (Mk 9:43), of the 'eternal punishment' in store for sinners (Mt 25:46), and Paul warns of 'the punishment of eternal destruction, separated from the presence of the Lord and from his glorious might' (2 Thess 1:9).

Sins and sinfulness

Throughout the bible, therefore, sin is taken seriously in all its aspects. It is not the mere transgression of a law, but a mysterious reality at work in the world, a dark power that can be overcome only by God himself, an evil that is finally conquered by the death of Christ. But this mysterious force is also described in terms of its concrete manifestations, in the sinful actions and omissions of individual men and of groups of people.

Though sin was always understood by the biblical writers as 'against the Lord', it was not restricted to religious failures in the narrow sense. It extended to all forms of selfishness, deceit, and exploitation. In the eighth century B.C. the prophet Amos was quite specific when, in the Lord's name, he castigated Israel for their sins: 'Listen to this, you that trample on the needy and try to destroy the poor of the country. You say to yourselves: 'We can hardly wait for the holy days to be over so that we can sell our corn. When will the sabbath end, so that we can start selling again?

Then we can overcharge, use false measures, and tamper with the scales to cheat our customers. We can sell worthless wheat at a high price. We'll find a poor man who can't pay his debts, not even the price of a pair of sandals, and we'll buy him as a slave' (Amos 8:4-6). Likewise, though the bible speaks of individual sinful actions, it lays more stress on the sinful attitudes behind them. Paul told the Colossians: 'You must put to death the earthly desires at work in you such as sexual immorality, indecency, lust, evil passions and greed (for greed is a form of idolatry)' (Col 3:5). Jesus made it quite clear that sin comes from the heart, that it is not a mere surface action: 'The things that come out of the mouth come from the heart, and these are the things that make a person unclean. For from his heart come the evil ideas which lead him to kill, commit adultery, and do other immoral things: to rob, lie and slander others' (Mt 15:18-19). Indeed, the greatest sin is the uncircumcised or stony heart, the hard, obdurate neck that makes people unteachable, impervious to God's call, insensitive to a neighbor's need.

Psychology of sin

The bible is also quite perceptive on the basic psychology of sin. The third chapter of Genesis, interpreted by Paul and succeeding generations of Christians as a description of the first, or original, sin, is really the story of every sin. The early chapters of Genesis tell us nothing about what happened at the beginning of time, but give us the religious meaning of what is happening all the time, not just to the first man, but to Everyman. We know nothing of the historical condition of the first human beings, but the paradise story describes God's plan for all men. He created us 'in his own image and likeness'. He shares with us his 'dominion over all the creatures of the earth'. He invites us to intimacy with him, wishes to treat us as friends who 'walk with him in the garden'. But we cannot be satisfied simply to accept his goodness, we want to be like him in deciding for ourselves what is good or evil. The one thing we cannot have, to be gods, is the one thing we want. This is the essence of all sin, to put self before God, to want something which is not ours, to want it so much that we ignore the consequences to ourselves or others. This, of course, is deception. We are blinded by our selfishness, and it is only afterwards that our eyes are opened, we discover that we are naked and have to hide, from God and from each other. Not only have we turned from God, but we are no longer at peace within ourselves, we are at odds with our neighbor and even the material world itself seems to turn sour on us.

The Vatican Council's document on the Church in the Modern World refers to this and relates it to every man's experience: 'Man abused his freedom at the very start of history. He lifted himself up against God and sought to attain his goal apart from him ... What revelation makes known to us is confirmed by our own experience. For when man looks into his own heart he finds that he is drawn towards what is wrong and sunk in many evils which cannot come from his good creator. Often refusing to acknowledge God as his source, man has also upset the relationship which should link him to his last end; and at the same time he has broken the right order that should reign within himself as well as between himself and other men and all creatures. Man, therefore, is divided within himself. As a result, the whole life of man, both individual and social, shows itself to be a struggle, and a dramatic one, between good and evil, between light and darkness (GS 13).

Historical development

This is the concept of sin we get from the bible: men's refusal to live according to God's plan, to behave as his children. Because of the special covenant of love which God had established with his chosen people, every deliberate failure to be fully human, to be hospitable, social and just was seen not simply as a misdemeanor, but as sin, as an offense against God himself. Of course, it would be an over-simplification to imagine that a theologically-refined notion of sin was present from the beginning, that the concept had no historical development. In fact, the Israelite understanding of sin developed in keeping with their notion of God. The Jewish people had a special experience of God as a personal being who consecrated them as his chosen ones: 'I am almighty God, obey me and always do what is right and I will make my covenant with you . . . I will keep my promise to you and to your descendants in future generations as an everlasting covenant. I will be your God' (Gen 17). This is clear from the earliest of the sacred writings. But, just as every adult still carries within him the infant and adolescent he once was, the Israelites down through the centuries continued to be influenced by more primitive notions of an autocratic, enforcing God, a rewarding and punishing God, a God more interested in his own laws and decrees than in people. Keeping the law brought the material reward of long life and wealth, while failure brought God's punishment in the form of poverty, misfortune, sickness and death. The modern version of this attitude is the Christian who avoids sin primarily because of the fear of hell, or who does good 'to get to heaven'. Besides, a shift of emphasis often took place. Since all laws (even of hygiene, social order and liturgical services) were interpreted as God's laws, the Jewish religion was in constant danger of being reduced to legalistic formalism: law for its own sake, the letter of the law even at the expense of its spirit.

In this context, sin became an offense against the law rather than a break in one's personal relationship with God. Though originally seen as God's will, God's word, mediating his love, the law at times became almost a barrier hiding the real God from men. Since one was perfect by the observance of the law, especially as interpreted by the Pharisees, all who did not follow Pharisaic observances were deemed sinners, and in the time of Christ the great majority of simple country people who could not understand or even remember those observances were considered beyond redemption. This attitude trivializes the whole notion of sin, divorces it from responsible morality. Jesus reacted strongly against this legalistic approach and condemned the Pharisees for straining at gnats and swallowing camels whole. Speaking of the sabbath observance, he reminded them that the law was made for men, not vice versa. Over-emphasis on law can stunt moral growth. There are still people today who see morality in terms of what is allowed or forbidden, who seldom ask why, who never wonder whether the laws in question are really God's law in the particular circumstances.

Moral codes in the bible?

This last point raises another important question with regard to what the bible has to say about sin. When there is question of 'God's law', we look to the bible as the revelation of God's will, expecting to find a code of revealed morality. God's own list of what is right and wrong. This over-simplified approach has led to no small confusion in contemporary discussion of moral issues. Biblical quotations are used as

arguments against, for example, masturbation, homosexuality and contraception, although it is quite clear
that the biblical writers had no conception of these
problems as understood today. This 'fundamentalist'
approach to scripture is not limited to ordinary Catholics, but is to be found even in official documents
of the Church.

The clearest and simplest example is in *Casti
Connubii*, Pope Pius XI's encyclical on marriage,
referring to Genesis 38. The text says: 'Those who,
in performing the conjugal act, deliberately deprive
it of its natural power and efficacy, act against nature
and do something which is shameful and intrinsically
immoral. We cannot wonder, then, if we find evidence
in the sacred scriptures that the Divine Majesty de-
tests this unspeakable crime with the deepest hatred
and has sometimes punished it with death, as St.
Augustine observes: 'Sexual intercourse even with a
lawful wife is unlawful and shameful if the conception
of offspring is prevented. This is what Onan, the son
of Juda, did, and on that account God put him to death'
(nn. 54-55). The text referred to here describes how
Onan, in fulfillment of the levirate law, should have
raised up children for his dead brother by sleeping
with his sister-in-law, but instead spilled his semen
on the ground every time he had intercourse with her.
Scripture scholars have long since shown that this
text says nothing about sexual morality as such; it
condemns Onan for his failure to carry out his duty to
his dead brother. It is interesting to note that none of
the more recent documents of the Holy See on the
same subject of contraception quote this scriptural
argument.

The mere fact that a particular practice is related
in the bible as 'God's law' does not mean that it is still
binding on today's Christians. In fact, those who quote
scriptural texts as the primary basis to approve or

condemn various kinds of human behavior today must read the bible very selectively. In the Genesis story, Onan is condemned by God for not doing what would be regarded today as immoral, namely having an adulterous relationship with his sister-in-law, Tamar. Furthermore, God's design in the story is realized by Tamar tempting her father-in-law into having inter-course with her by pretending to be a prostitute. This is only one of the many cases in the bible where incest, fornication, polygamy, deceit, etc. are presented as part of the divine plan. The same chapter of Deu-teronomy which formulates the levirate law obliging a man to sleep with the wife of his dead brother and produce children for him, also has Moses, in God's name, commanding: 'If two men are having a fight and the wife of one tries to help her husband by grabbing hold of the other man's genitals, show her no mercy; cut off her hand' (Deut 25:11).

Even in the matter of obedience there is a bible text which is revolting to a modern Christian conscience. As lawgiver speaking in God's name, Moses com-mands: 'Suppose a man has a son who is stubborn and rebellious, a son who will not obey his parents, even though they punish him. His parents are to take him before the leaders of the town where he lives and make him stand trial. They are to say to them: 'Our son is stubborn and rebellious and refuses to obey us; he wastes money and is a drunkard.' Then the men of the city are to stone him to death, and so you will get rid of this evil. Everyone in Israel will hear what has happened and be afraid' (Deut 21:18-21).

The ten commandments

Of course, common sense will immediately see that these barbaric precepts can in no way be accepted as 'God's law'. But the traditionally-minded will go on to explain that we must distinguish between man-made laws which reflect the mentality of a particular age and culture (like those just quoted) and the revealed law of God as expressed in the ten commandments. Certainly, there are distinctions to be made between the meaning and importance of different biblical texts, but it does not follow that we can find in the bible a code of 'revealed morality' handed down by God himself, a list of moral laws directly revealed. Most people are aware that the story of Moses being given the stone tablets containing the decalogue on Mount Sinai is not to be taken literally, but how many realize that, in terms of material content, most of the ten commandments were widely known centuries earlier by non-Israelite peoples, and were the common law of Mesopotamia? In formulating the decalogue, the Israelites drew on the accumulated wisdom of the surrounding peoples as well as on their own experience. Their laws reflect popular morality of the time, and derive from a variety of circumstances and backgrounds. Scripture scholars tell us that in the early history of Israel, the common law concerning the institution of marriage was not very different from what it was in the neighboring civilizations. Polygamy, legalized concubinage, divorce prevailed there as elsewhere. There was no sociological break with the rest of the ancient Near East. The only real distinction was the specifically religious one, the basic values of the society and its understanding of God.

This applies also to the new testament. Jesus left no detailed code of morality, so Paul and the early Christian communities simply fell back on the moral codes current at the time, which happened to come from the Stoic philosophers. The lists of virtues and vices in Paul's letters are largely the household rules common in his day (Col 3:18-4:1; Ephes 5:22-6:9; I Cor

6:9-10). What is special to Paul and the other new
testament writers is the new context in which they
presented these lists. The vices and virtues then current in the Greek world were used to describe what is
opposed to 'life in the Spirit' and what are the fruits
of the Spirit for one who is 'in Christ' (Gal 5:1,2,6,
16-25). The new testament, therefore, cannot give us a
direct and simple answer to modern problems like the
oil crisis, inflation and poverty, racial conflict, ecol-
ogy, social justice, birth control, homosexuality.

Insights from scripture

The question then arises: if it is a mistake to go to the
bible for 'new bits of morality', specific moral laws
directly revealed by God, how are we to use sacred
scripture in our understanding of morality, or why
bother with the bible at all? There are many things
we find in scripture to inspire and enlighten us in
deciding moral issues: God's fatherhood and the con-
sequent brotherhood of all men; the goodness of creation; the world entrusted to man's responsibility;
God's care for all, especially the weak; the dignity
of each human person, created in the image and likeness of God; God's patience and never-ending forgiveness; the example of Jesus in his relation to the Father
and in his total availability to men; his attitude to
evil and his acceptance of the cross; the sermon on the
mount; the beatitudes; God's will for the salvation
of all men. Any number of insights or themes can be
gleaned from the bible to influence us in our approach
to moral problems, to sensitize us to certain values,
to color our outlook and attitude to daily life. We can
also be enlightened and helped by studying how the
people of God in times past dealt with particular
problems, in both old and new testaments. But their
solutions cannot be the last word for us. In the bible

we can find some concern about fundamental human values, the same values to which we ourselves subscribe. But something else altogether is the bible's description of historically dated attempts to enshrine these values in laws for human behavior.

The values are still meaningful and binding, but some of the laws embodying them have little meaning in today's world. Even the values themselves have undergone a change in many cases. For example, we still think that hospitality is a high moral value, but we shrink from the way Lot sacrificed his daughters for the sake of it. When the men of Sodom wanted to have their way with his two visitors, Lot entreated them: 'Friends, don't do such a wicked thing. Look, I have two daughters who are still virgins. Let me bring them out to you, and you can do whatever you want with them. But don't do anything to these men; they are guests in my house, and I must protect them (Gen 19:7-8). These changes of attitude and understanding are not arbitrary, but are part of the normal process of human growth. From the time of Abraham or Jesus to our own day, there has been considerable development in the conscience of mankind, without extra bits of directly revealed moral knowledge. The prophets could summon the people of God to a holy war to exterminate enemies, including women and children, and Paul would be surprised at our modern abhorrence of slavery. But today's Christians cannot afford to feel too superior, since we still have a long way to go in acknowledging in practice the full human rights of women.

Why quote Paul to the effect that homosexuals are excluded from the kingdom of heaven (e.g. I Cor 6:9), and forget that the bible also says that 'Women are not to wear men's clothing, and men are not to wear women's clothing; the Lord your God hates people who do such things' (Deut 21:5)? This is not meant as petty criticism of the biblical writers, but simply to make the point that the word of the bible alone cannot give us God's revealed solution to a moral problem. People become confused when preachers label things as sins on the basis of a few words from scripture, and they feel disloyal and guilty when they are tempted to criticize the preacher or the Church. We are simply asking the wrong question when we ask: what does God say? and then search scripture for the appropriate quotation. In fact, Jesus himself rejected the formal authority of the scriptures as absolutely binding. Interpreting scripture for his hearers, he did not treat it like other rabbis, drawing out its every implication, but instead opposed one passage with another to show what God's will meant in the present. The people of God in the old testament were not handed a code of morality from heaven, but had to discover and formulate it in the course of their experience, according to the varying circumstances of their lives. They refined and perfected it through the centuries. At times it lagged behind that of their pagan neighbors in some respects, while in others it reflected a more refined moral sense. The essential difference between their code and that of their neighbors was not that one was revealed and the other not. In terms of material content, they were practically the same. The distinguishing feature of the Jewish decalogue was its religious meaning and context. For the Israelites, the ten commandments were not simply the rules for peaceful living in community, but the consequence of their being specially chosen by God, their response to his loving initiative in making them his chosen people. The commandments were the concrete expression of the way of life implied in the covenant situation of the whole people of Israel. In this context, the people came to see them, not as discovered by human wisdom through the ages, but as God's gift to them, and in that sense 'revealed'.

Bible not the last word

The commandments themselves are quite general and flexible. They were sufficient for the needs of a simple nomadic people. But with the growing complexities of agricultural and town life, they needed to be further spelled out. Hence the proliferation of old testament laws. But these laws all reflected the circumstances and understanding of their times. Thus, for example, some of the laws governing sexuality are more con-cerned with justice, with the rights of husband and father, than with sexual life as such, and they consider the woman more a possession of man than a person in her own right. The same is true of the new testa-ment. Many of its moral precepts are colored by the culture of the period. Our task is to disentangle the basic Christian attitudes and principles from the particular form in which they are embodied and presented. Jesus did not leave a detailed code of morality, and the new testament writers did not adhere rigidly to the letter of what he said. Rather, they interpreted, adapted and applied his sayings to new situations. The early Christian communities had to formulate their own specific moral rules in the light of the new life in Christ which they believed they were called to live. The life and words of Jesus would always be a special challenge and example, but faith in him could never dispense his followers from the continuing search for God's will in the concrete. The same is true today. A bible quotation can never solve a moral problem or end a discussion. The Christian community of today may get special help from the words of scripture, both old and new testaments. It

will be enlightened, encouraged and strengthened
by the presence of the Risen Christ and his Spirit in its
midst. But it still has to discover the appropriate rules
to meet new situations and needs, to discern God's
will in the present.

Sin outside the Church

The question: what does the bible say about sin? could
give the impression that sin is a reality only for believers. This is not the case. Sin is a reality for all
men, just as redemption and grace are for all men. The
word is not used apart from a religious context, so
unbelievers do not normally describe evildoing as
sin. Without belief in a personal God, they cannot
see that their misdeeds are a break in the relationship
with him. But it does not follow that the reality covered by the word 'sin' has no place in their lives. They
are all part of God's plan of salvation. The bible tells
us of God's infinite love for all men. To make explicit
his plan for mankind, he chose a special people to be
the vehicle of his revelation and self-gift. In the old
testament he chose a handful of nomads and fashioned
them into a people, a close-knit community whom he
set apart and consecrated for himself. They in turn
consecrated themselves to him by accepting to be his
people as he was their God. In founding his church,
Christ renewed the covenant God had made with his
people, in fact made a new covenant, so that the
Church is the new people of God. The Christian community is a people consecrated by God in baptism,
specially marked and set aside for a purpose in the
world — to be his witnesses, a sacrament or sign of his
presence among men, not just a sign pointing elsewhere, but an efficacious sign making his presence a
here-and-now reality for those who believe. Christians respond to this call by consecrating themselves

to him, accepting the challenge to be his witnesses, to try to reproduce in the world something of the life of Christ himself, individually and in community.

But the difference between them and the rest of humanity is not that God is present to them and not to the others, that they have grace and salvation denied to outsiders. The difference, rather, is between explicit and implicit. God is doing explicitly in the Church what he is doing implicitly in the world at large. There is no world of 'mere nature', cut off from the supernatural world of God. God and his love and salvation are involved in the whole world of mankind. In the depths of their conscience, all men are called to be good, to be fully human, to grow into the fullness of the maturity of Christ. Christians know this explicitly. Others hear it implicitly in the moral demands of their conscience, and they have the freedom to accept or reject it. To the extent that they respond to this call in fidelity to their conscience, that they go beyond their own selfishness and reach out to others in genuine concern, they are implicitly responding to God and thus growing in the Christ-life, even though the circumstances of their lives may cut them off from any explicit knowledge of God or Christ. Their moral consciousness can develop to a point at which it passes implicitly into religious consciousness, even without their being aware of it. Thus, there can be an implicit awareness of the divine reality even in some persons who profess themselves atheists. Such people are often called 'anonymous Christians'. Their morally good behavior, therefore, is a growth in Christ and grace, and their evil deeds are sins, though of course they themselves would not describe them as such.

In our discussion of the various factors affecting people's notion of sin in the following chapters, we

confine ourselves to those who have a religious context to give meaning to the term. But this should not
allow us to forget that nonbelievers can sin and are
caught up in the mystery of sin in the world. On the
other hand, we need to be reminded that if we speak
of 'anonymous Christians' in the world outside the
Church, there are also a number of 'anonymous pagans' in the midst of our Christian communities. If
'belief' is to be measured by real commitment to Christ
and his gospel rather than by pious practices and
mere surface attachment to a Church, the line between
belief and unbelief may pass through each one of us
rather than between classes of people. For that matter,
the line between saint and sinner is not simply a
division between two groups, but passes through
each individual heart, since each one of us is a bit of
both. This should cause no surprise, since every
Christian is a sinner who is called to be a saint.

3

IS IT ALLOWED?

Until quite recently the catechism definition of sin was: any thought, word or deed contrary to the law of God. One of the most widely-used summaries of moral theology, still being reprinted in the sixties, introduced the chapter on sin with the statements: 'Sin is the free transgression of a divine law. Every law is, in a sense, a derivation from the divine law; therefore, the transgression of any law is sinful.' It is no wonder that for many people morality is often restricted to legality, that right and wrong are understood in terms of what is allowed and what is forbidden. This infantile attitude was, if not created, at least encouraged, by much of the church's moralistic preaching. Textbooks of moral theology used precisely the kind of language that emphasized law as the primary criterion of morality, the measure of right and wrong. The following quotations are just a few examples: 'The direct taking of one's own life is a *mortal sin* if done on one's own authority. It is also *forbidden* to do something from which death will accidentally follow, if one has suicidal intentions in doing it, e.g. to smoke or drink immoderately in order to shorten one's life. Indirect suicide is in itself *forbidden,* but may be *permitted* for a proportionately grave reason.' 'Self-mutilation is *allowed* only to save one's life.' 'Dangerous tight-rope walking, etc. merely for motives of gain or vanity is *forbidden,* though if practice or skill make the danger remote there would be *no mortal sin* in such action.' With regard to the obligation of Sunday rest, the same text lists the *forbidden* servile works, and goes on to say that 'custom justifies shaving, haircutting, knitting, etc., and it is *also permitted* to go walking, riding, driving, rowing, journeying, even though these be very fatiguing.' Another textbook uses the same language when speaking of the sixth commandment: 'It is *permitted* to take baths, to wash oneself, to mount a horse, etc., even if one foresees a possible pollution. In the same manner it is *permitted* to scratch an irritation of the genital region provided that the itching does not proceed from an excess of semen or the heat of passion. When the cause of the irritation is in doubt, scratching is *permitted*. If the irritation is slight, it is *permitted* to scratch even when the scratching may provoke slight sexual stirrings.'

Danger of law

With such an emphasis not only on law as such, but on the multiplicity of laws attempting to cover every conceivable situation, it is no wonder that many of today's Catholics are confused about the notion of sin. There have been so many changes in the church in recent years that people are no longer sure what is allowed and what is forbidden. Concerned parents (and not only those over thirty) complain that their children are no longer taught what is sinful and what is not, and that the commandments are seldom mentioned in religion classes. Some preachers are at a loss to explain the church's laws in today's world, and long for the black-and-white precision of the older approach. But this attitude to law is no longer sufficient for an understanding of morality and sin.

Certainly, law is an essential element in Christian morality, and sin is a breaking of God's law. 'Keep the law, and the law will keep you' has a certain attractiveness, and generations of good people have led holy lives with this simple attitude. It makes life easy and straightforward. You know where you stand. All important decisions are made for you in advance; there is no doubt, indecision or agony of conscience. It also makes for uniformity; everybody is bound by the same law, with no messy exceptions. The good Catholic is easily recognized as the one who keeps the laws of the church. The church itself is clearly marked off from other Christian groups by its distinctive rules and regulations. Shortly before the Council, it was commonly quoted with pride that the Catholic church had been given an exceptionaly high rating for its efficiency as an organization by an international firm of business consultants. A good system of laws can make for order, stability and efficiency in society, and the morally good person is normally a law-abiding citizen.

Sin and law

But an exaggerated emphasis on law gave rise to serious inadequacies in people's understanding of morality and Christian living. When sin is primarily seen as the transgression of a law, it is easy to feel that where there is no clearcut law there can be no question of sin, indeed no moral obligation at all. For example, there are people who confess to having missed Sunday Mass, even though they were sick and unable to attend. Although their illness excused them, they still feel obligation and a certain amount of guilt because of the specific law. On the other hand, their marriage could be falling apart because of some personality disorder recognized as the cause of their trouble, but they would not see any sin in their failing to get professional help, because there is no law to the effect that they should see a marriage counsellor on the first Monday after discovering their problem. Again, a person may confess to having used contraceptives, but fail to realize that sin, and indeed serious sin, may be involved in his savage driving habits, his dangerous parking on a corner, his flirting with people at work, his lack of sensitivity towards his wife, his failure to give time to his children, his obsession with his job or hobby. A priest may accuse himself of not praying his breviary, but see no sin in his authoritarian attitudes to parishioners, his frequent failure to respect their intelligence or experience as he talks down to them from the pulpit, never listens to them, and generally behaves as though he owned the parish. All sin is idolatry, setting oneself up as the center of one's world, suiting self without regard for God, for neighbors, for consequences. But in practice most sin consists in simply *not bothering* about patience, kindness, humility, temperance, discretion. There is no precise law about these things, so people are inclined to regard them as optional extras reserved for those striving for perfection.

Over-emphasis on law also tended to reduce morality to mere obedience, so that little room was left for conscience and personal responsibility. All one needed was to discover the appropriate law for each situation and assess how far it was binding in the circumstances. Since this was the only exercise of conscience that many people were familiar with, it is hardly surprising that they are confused, and feel let down when confessors now tell them that they must 'follow their conscience' on a question where the law is a matter of controversy, as in the birth control issue.

When law becomes paramount in morality, the church as a whole suffers. The church is a very large institution, and like every institution it cannot survive without law. But when law takes pride of place, the church tends to be identified with the institution and people lose sight of the fact that it is equally a

fraternity of brothers and sisters in the Lord, a sacrament of Christ, a herald of the kingdom of God, and a
servant of the world that Jesus came to save. These are
more than just titles. They are the reality of the
church, and the church needs to be _experienced_ in
these ways by its members. But pre-occupation with
law can block that experience. Over-concern with
law is most damaging to pastors and bishops, who can
become simply administrators hiding behind the law
whenever a difficulty arises and refusing to dialog
with a brother in distress.

Appreciation of law

Law can become impersonal, and its observance
mechanical and empty. But its inadequacies and
dangers should not lead us to a total rejection of it.
For true religion and service to God, we need a real
appreciation of it, combined with a critical awareness
of its limitations and pitfalls. To savor it in its proper
religious context, one should read psalm 119, the
longest psalm in the bible. Almost every one of its
hundred and seventy six verses is in praise of God's
law, of its goodness and power, and of the protection
it affords: 'Happy are those who live according to the
law of the Lord . . . I will obey your laws . . . I take
pleasure in your laws; your commands I will not
forget . . . Open my eyes that I may see the wonderful
truths in your law . . . Explain your law to me and I will
obey it; I will keep it with all my heart . . . Your word,
O Lord, will last forever; it is eternal in heaven . . . The
rules that you have given are completely fair and
right . . . I will always praise you, because you teach
me your law . . .' This was the attitude of the early
Israelites to law. It was not seen as a burden nor a
an arbitrary imposition by a remote and angry God,

but as a privilege and a gift revealed by the God who loved them. To obey it was to be faithful to the covenant, to prosper and be happy, to share in God's wisdom. In the law, God was offering himself, and therefore offering wisdom and life. The law was wisdom, the knowledge of how true life was to be lived. The response was not so much to learn the law in all its details, as to accept God, to love and serve him with one's whole heart and mind in the concrete circumstances of daily life. As these circumstances varied through the centuries, the law changed and developed. It became a living tradition guiding and directing the people's response to God. The details were gleaned from experience and many of the formulations were copied from the surrounding peoples, but these were always incorporated into a context that lifted them onto a new level, the religious level of the people of God.

Legalism

With such high regard for the law, however, it was not easy to avoid the temptation to legalism and formalism. The law which was meant to be a free response to God, a share in his wisdom, often became an end in itself. It was looked on as God's word, revealing God's mind. But in the attitude of some, it actually became God's mind itself, then took on an objective life of its own within God's mind, and finally outside and even above God's mind. A jewish rabbinical tradition at the time of Jesus maintained that the law was so sacred that even God himself studied it for a certain length of time each day. When the law became fixed in a canonical legal text, the temptation to absolutize and make it an end in itself became all the greater. The law was so sacred that no prophet, no new Moses could change or replace it. In practice, the law was God, more immediate and more concrete than the real God. The Lawgiver became bound, circumscribed by his own law. All of God was expressed in the law, he became reduced to the law. For the Jewish people, this was the letter at the expense of the spirit. The law had been given to make them free, with the freedom of the children of God. But they used it to avoid the complexity of life and the pain of decision. They abdicated their power to make personal moral decisions. The law decided all questions in advance; they had only to obey. The law was no longer valued because of its relation to God and the covenant, but because the people could rely on it, measure it, obey it and be in the clear before God. This was boasting and complacency. This was the attitude for which Jesus castigated the pharisees. Likewise, when Paul inveighed against the law, it was not so much against the specific details of its content as against the place accorded it by the Jews, as though they could be justified by the law.

This was a constant danger throughout the whole of the old testament. The prophets continually warned against it, and in the liturgical ceremonies for the renewal of the covenant the people were reminded of the kind of God who had chosen them, and the kind of service he required. They were told that true religion was a matter of the heart, and that the Lord wanted worshippers in spirit and in truth. But the very multiplicity of legislation tended to exaggerate its importance. It is easy to criticize the scribes and pharisees for their six hundred and thirteen precepts, and forget that the Christian church has continued the tradition, and in some ways outstripped the pharisees, both in the multiplication of its laws and in the intricacies of its casuistry. The canon law of the Catholic church has almost two and a half thousand separately numbered pieces of legislation in its code, not to mention supplementary rules in other documents. No society can survive without some organization, and the larger the society the more complex its body of law. The simple structures that kept the first Christians together would not suffice for today's six hundred million Catholics. But somewhere along the line a serious shift of emphasis took place as law developed. Laws which were formulated to guide people in their response to God often reached a stage where they defeated their purpose and became a positive obstacle.

Defeating its purpose

There are hundreds of examples, but a few will suffice. There is a Christian obligation to pray, and over the centuries the church developed the divine office in latin, originally for choral recitation in the monasteries, but eventually imposed on all in sacred orders. The seriousness of the obligation was such that it was considered a mortal sin, punishable by an eternity in hell, to omit even three short psalms from it. Until the early sixties one could not fulfill the obligation by praying the office in English; it had to be in latin to avoid mortal sin. This applied even to nuns who did not understand a word they were saying. One wonders how many of these good sisters and priests ever suspected that Jesus was trying to tell us something when he commanded: 'When you pray, do not use a lot of meaningless words, as the pagans do, who think that God will hear them because their prayers are long' (Mt 6:7). Since the obligation was to 'say' the office, it could not be fulfilled unless the vocal chords actually vibrated, even though no sound was heard. It was further explained that internal attention was not necessary for the essence of prayer, and that the obligation could be fulfilled even though the prayer was said with freely willed distractions. What a far cry from the teaching of Jesus (Mt 6:5-13).

Similarly, to promote reverence for the blessed eucharist and dispose people to receive it, the church imposed the law of total fast from midnight, again, under pain of mortal sin. As social conditions changed, people found this more and more difficult, until a stage was reached where, until about twenty years ago, the vast majority of Mass-going Catholics abstained from communion, except on rare occasions. The law was so absolute that even the accidental swallowing of a drop of water while brushing one's teeth was enough to bar one from communion. In explaining the law, it was pointed out that the eucharistic fast could be broken by sucking a drop of blood from a pin-prick or a bleeding gum, but not by biting one's nails, because the latter were not edible, and could not be counted as food. The current legislation has a one-hour fast, and not a few people spend most of the Mass praying fervently that the service will be delayed or prolonged sufficiently to complete the hour since their last meal, so that they can communicate.

Pharisees not dead

Catholics under thirty will not remember those days and may well be puzzled by it all, but the older generation can recall how scrupulously such laws were observed. They were intended to be helpful, but were enforced far beyond the point where help becomes a hindrance. Loyalty to the church may prompt one to point out the good intention of the legislators and the efforts of commentators to be helpful to people, but one can be forgiven for wondering if this is what religion is all about. The above examples are only a small sample of what was taken for granted as normal; one could easily quote a large number of others that are far more incredible. Law had become such an absolute in the church that the vast majority of the faithful, beginning with bishops and priests, were simply not aware of how faithfully we were following in the footsteps of the scribes and pharisees excoriated by Jesus.

We are so accustomed to the bad press this class of people are given in the gospels that we forget that they were the religious establishment of the time. The scribes were the lawyers, moralists and theologians of the Jewish community to which Jesus belonged. They were the guides and teachers who spent their lives 'searching the scriptures'. The pharisees were a middle-class religious party noted for their exact observance of the Mosaic law and of the 'traditions of the elders'. When the law of Moses forbade work on the sabbath, 'work' had to be defined, so there were thirty-nine basic actions listed as forbidden, including carrying a burden, reaping, winnowing, threshing and preparing a meal. People wanted to know what constituted a 'burden', so it was decided that anything weighing the equivalent of two dried figs came under the ban. When the disciples of Jesus plucked the ears of corn on the sabbath, they were guilty of several infringements of the sabbath law (Mt 12). By plucking the corn they were guilty of reaping; rubbing it in their hands was threshing, separating grain and chaff was winnowing, and the whole process was preparing a meal. No wonder the pharisees condemned them.

But why should we self-righteously applaud when we read of Jesus castigating the pharisees, and fail to see that in many ways we are no different? The church loses credibility when we insist that of course there is a difference, even if it cannot be seen. A little humility and realism would be much more becoming to the Christian community. The command of Moses against setting up idols, and the words of Jesus about law being for man and not vice versa, are not simply for the Jews of the exodus or of first-century Palestine. They are for God's people in every age, including our own. It would be unchristian arrogance to claim that we have no need of such warnings, that we are above temptation.

Confusion about law

Our reaction to the exaggeration of the past, however, should not be a rejection of law, but a better understanding of its true meaning and the purpose it serves in human living. But this is where the confusion starts, because we hear of God's law and human law, natural law and positive law, church law and civil law, and few of the faithful ever have an opportunity of getting clear answers to their questions. What is law all about? In what sense is it God's law? Is it really a sin to break a law?

First of all, we need to see the context from which law get its meaning. Man is a social being. He not only has a capacity for relating to other people, but he needs them. People need people, nobody grows alone. But if people are allowed to simply bump against each other in a group, pandemonium will follow and nobody will grow. If the physical, emotional, intellectual and spiritual needs of individuals are to be met even on a minimal level, there is need for community, for stability and predictability in the community, for role-definition, and for the recognition of certain rights and obligations. This is what laws are for. Any group of people, if they are to live and work together, soon discover the need for laws to regulate their relationships, so each community formulates the rules it needs.

Positive law

Individuals born in the community, and outsiders coming in, find an already established pattern of behavior in the community, regulated by traditions and customs, and in modern society by written constitutions and laws. Thus, most people experience law as an imposition from without, something decided and established by an authority external to themselves, demanding obedience. This is commonly called 'positive law', a regulation of human behavior positively formulated and enacted by the lawful authority for a particular community. Its purpose is to protect basic human rights and freedoms: the right to life, to bodily integrity, to property; freedom of movement, expression and association. It regulates conflicting interests, so that the common good of all will be served. It seems to limit freedom insofar, for example, as it imposes traffic regulations involving red lights and speed limits. But such limitation of freedom provides safety which in the long run makes for greater freedom for all concerned. This element of limitation may reinforce people's feeling that law is imposed from without. But reflection will show that positive laws are not arbitrary, that most members of the community, if they had to reflect on the needs of the situation, would agree, not only to law as such, but also to the limitations on their freedom, in their own interest and in the interest of all. There is an element of arbitrariness insofar as it makes little difference to the smooth running of traffic whether people drive on the left or the right, but it is recognized that a decision must be made in favor of one or the other to avoid chaos. By having specific laws, carefully formulated and systematically enforced, people are freed from the necessity of deciding at every step what is the best thing to be done.

Without such laws, each individual would have to discover for himself the best course of action on every occasion, which would involve considerable time spent in collecting and assessing all the facts of the situation, calculating the short-term and long-term results on himself and on others of each possible decision. Not everybody would be in a position to know all the facts, or have the experience to evaluate them correctly, or foresee the possible consequences. Nor can we be sure that each one would be sufficiently free of selfishness to think of others and the common good. By formulating a law to be obeyed by all, the community frees the individual members from the burden of such decision-making in a variety of matters, thus freeing them for the ordinary business of living. To live in a law-abiding society where the laws are just, is to experience a high degree of freedom: freedom from the fear of bodily assault and the various forms of exploitation, freedom to travel safely, to possess property and provide for one's future and one's children, freedom to develop one's potential and to grow as a person.

Values before law

It is because people value freedom, order, stability, justice, bodily health, safety, community living, etc. that they enact and accept laws to promote, guarantee and protect these values. The laws themselves may be felt as an imposition and a burden, but the values they enshrine or protect correspond to our basic needs as human beings. We may grumble at the tax laws, but we do really want the social services provided by our tax money. It is _values_, therefore, which are primary. Laws are secondary or derivative. The kind of laws needed for the safeguarding and promotion of a particular value will vary according to the culture and living conditions of the community. Laws governing taxation and traffic are an obvious example. But even more basic laws can change. For example, human life has always been regarded as a value with a high priority, but respect for life can give rise to very different laws. Thus, in primitive societies subject to frequent attack from enemies, the sick and elderly were put to death by relatives and members of their own tribe. This was not disrespect for life, but to save them from a worse fate at the hands of the enemy, and to save the healthy members from being slowed down in their flight and therefore killed by having to care for the weaker ones. Likewise, in some tribes, a foreigner was considered an enemy, a potential attacker, and it was judged lawful to kill him, a kind of self-defense in anticipation. In our more settled conditions, however, we have laws against euthanasia, foreigners are not killed as enemies, and more and more the death penalty is seen as an inadequate response by the community to lawbreakers.

Besides, not only will respect for the same basic value give rise to different laws through time, but even the values themselves change. There are no values in the abstract. Values exist only in people's minds. They are what people consider worthwhile, what they are prepared to live for, to sacrifice their time, effort and money for. Mankind has changed considerably in the course of history, and so people grow in their appreciation of basic values, and discover new ones. Thus, the notion of human freedom and dignity strikes a deeper chord in modern hearts than it did in earlier centuries. Slavery could be accepted without question by St. Paul and even defended philosophically by St. Thomas Aquinas, whereas the very idea of slavery is abhorrent to people today. It is obvious, therefore, that even values themselves have a history, that they are not static or absolute. It is only recently that people realized that respect for human dignity involves recognizing sexual equality between men and women, and we still have some distance to go before this recognition is reflected in our laws.

God's law?

At this point, one might ask: what has all this got to do with sin? The theology text-book quoted at the beginning of this chapter defined sin as the free transgression of a divine law and went on to explain that all law derives from the law of God. Popular preaching often gave the impression that over and above 'human law', as described above, there is a special 'divine law' revealed by God, and that human law is unjust, not true law, not binding in conscience if it in any way contradicts God's law. There is indeed a sense in which this is true, as we shall see shortly. But the impression large numbers of people have, is that there is a 'law of God' that can be consulted and read off in much the same way as one would look up a point of civil or ecclesiastical legislation. There is an idea of 'God's law' in many people's minds which is at the root of much of the confusion in discussions of morality and sin. Since God is eternal, immutable, all-wise, his law must likewise be eternal, unchanging, perfect. It is frequently described as 'absolute', therefore binding in all circumstances and admitting of no exceptions.

There are a number of difficulties about such a view. First of all, there is no 'revealed law of God' in the sense of a specific, formulated law communicated directly by God to any man or group of men. The older theology books used to present the ten commandments in this way as a revelation to Moses. Theologians explained that apart from the command to keep the sabbath holy (a positive law of God), all the others were precepts of 'natural law', which could be discovered by unaided human reason. But since they could be discovered only with great difficulty, and yet are so necessary for man's moral life, God revealed them directly to the human race through Moses. This view rested on a very literal understanding of the bible that cannot be accepted today. Not only do we know that the content of the decalog in general predates Moses, but we recall the many culturally-determined, and to our modern mind, rather barbaric practices, that were proclaimed in the old testament as the 'law of God'. Nowhere in the bible can we find a single specific law 'revealed' directly by God, much less can we look on old or new testaments as a handbook or code of revealed morality. Jesus gave us a 'new law', that we love each other as he loves us, but he left it to us to discover what true love means in different situations, and what it demands of us in practice. It is a principle of action, an ideal to inspire us, but not a law as such. Neither the 'law of Christ', nor the example of the life of Christ, nor any of the words of Christ will tell the conscientious doctor when to cease prolonging the life of an incurably ill patient.

Official pronouncements of the church on moral matters frequently invoke the 'divine law', and state that certain things are against the 'law of God'. Most Catholics who got beyond the elementary stages of the catechism were told that the commandments of the church were ecclesiastical laws, therefore human laws. Human law was explained as an ordinance of human reason for the common good promulgated by the lawful authority: civil law for the civil society of the state, and ecclesiastical law for the religious society which is the church. But divine law is a higher law, a more basic law, the foundation on which both civil and church laws depend. It was recognized that ecclesiastical laws, the ordinary legislation of the church, could change from time to time, that one could be given a dispensation from them, and that in certain circumstances they were not binding (e.g. the Sunday Mass obligation during illness). But the 'divine law' was unchangeable, absolute, allowing no exceptions, and could not be abrogated or dispensed from, even by the Vicar of Christ himself, since a vicar cannot over-rule the will of his sovereign.

However, we have the same difficulty with the documents of the church as with the bible itself. They contain no evidence of a specific, formulated law re-vealed by God to any authority in the church. They also have the other difficulty noticed in the biblical references to 'God's law', namely that in spite of the divine law being unchanging and absolute, it is sur-prising the number of things the church claimed to be against the 'law of God' that have changed or been quietly dropped throughout the centuries. Pope Leo X declared, against Luther, that the burning of heretics is fully in accordance with the will of the Holy Spirit. If this is really the case, then the present Holy Father would be bound to subscribe to the same treatment, even though he might prefer not to shout it from the housetops or try to bring pressure to bear on civil governments to allow him to put it into practice.

Natural law

Does it follow, therefore, that there is no such thing as a 'law of God'? Yes, if we mean a set of specific laws already formulated, needing only to be read off as occasion requires. There are no such laws in the bible, nor in church documents. If we claim that they exist in God's mind, we have the problem of discovering them, because God's mind is not immediately open to our inspection. Nevertheless, throughout the ages, men have always appealed to a justice higher than law and against which all human law must be judged. It is spoken of as the unwritten law, the natural moral law, the law of God. St. Paul says that the gentiles have this law written in their hearts (Rom 2:15). In a very real sense, therefore, there is a 'law of God'. Man is not a law unto himself, the sole arbiter of right and wrong, but is dependent on God, his creator. In the physical world about him, he discovers a whole series of laws built into the very nature of things, the laws of physics, chemistry, biology, etc. Insofar as he formulates his discoveries into laws, they are simply a description of the internal structure of the universe which man can come to know more accurately with the progress of science, but which he has not the power to change. These laws (e.g. gravity, aerodynamics, the laws of plant, animal or human reproduction) simply describe the nature of things, the way things are and behave. Man himself is part of this created world, and is subject to the same laws insofar as he is a physical and living being. These are simply the laws of nature, not a moral law. But man is a special kind of living being. He is capable not only of seeing how things *are,* but because of his powers of conceptual thought and free choice, he also knows how things *might* be, and in some cases how things *ought* to be. When it comes to painting his house, for example, he can freely choose from a variety of colors. His final choice may be a matter of personal taste and preference. But in his dealings with his fellowmen, his choice of action will be influenced by an awareness of the fact that he *ought* not to deceive, exploit or murder them.

This awareness will have come to him through the laws explicitly formulated by the community (e.g. the ten commandments). But to the extent that he has reached some degree of moral maturity, he will be convinced that behind the particular law, there is a basic human value at stake, a value he must respect if he is to be true to his nature. He will have experienced some basic need in his own nature which must be met if he is to grow as a person. There are physiological needs (food, warmth, etc), safety needs, the need to love and be loved, to belong, to have roots in a community, to be esteemed by his fellowmen, to be self-determining and self-actualizing. The meeting of these needs brings satisfaction and fulfillment as a person, so down through the centuries society has formulated laws to ensure that they will be met. Since these laws are determined by the basic needs of human nature itself, and not the eccentricities of isolated individuals, they are referred to as the 'natural' moral law, the law governing human behavior based on the very nature of man. Since man does not create his own nature, but discovers it already shaped by God, with its in-built needs and direction, the natural moral law is often described as 'God's law'. Since we cannot read God's mind directly to discover his law, we can find it reflected in his creation, in the same way that we can guess the blueprint in an inventor's mind by studying the machine he produced.

Blueprint theory

This 'blueprint' or 'maker's instructions' theory of natural law has given rise to misunderstanding and is responsible for much of the confusion in contemporary discussions of moral issues. Because the 'nature of man' can be studied and described in the

same way as the nature of animals, plants or non-
living things, the natural moral law is often compared
to the laws of physics, chemistry, physiology, etc. —
clear, fixed, stable, needing only to be 'discovered'
in man's nature. But this is to leave out of account
the most distinctive feature of human nature, man's
creative intelligence and free will. Though man's basic
needs remain the same, his nature is not something
static and fixed for all time. Man is a being of possibilities, and he creates his nature as he decides among
these possibilities. Inwardly, he changes each time
he adopts a new image of himself or gets a new understanding of himself. For example, his understanding
of his body, of his sexuality, or of his relationship
to the material universe is radically different from
what it was in primitive times. Outwardly, he changes
insofar as he fashions instruments to become extensions of himself and change the world he inhabits.
Many of his inventions bring about a whole new civilization, though it may not be realized at the time. Thus,
printing was first thought to be merely a new way of
reproducing books, and the motor-car just a faster
means of travel, but both of these inventions trans-
formed society, and in a sense the very nature of man
himself. Thus, change is an essential part of man's
unchanging nature. It is a mistake to imagine that God
created an original human nature at the beginning
of time, to which any subsequent development must
be considered an addition, something almost artificial.

    This fundamentalist understanding of human
nature tends to give an exaggerated importance to
man's physical and biological nature in determining
moral norms. The impression is given that we can best
discover God's plan for man by studying the human
functions in their natural state, prior to any inter-
vention by man himself. Thus, speech is for communi-
cating knowledge, eating for the conservation of

health, sex for reproduction. But this approach ignores the fact that these activities are *human*, and have their full human meaning only in a human context, which includes intelligence, free will and the whole world of culture. The laws governing these activities insofar as they are physical are not moral laws. They tell us nothing about how these activities are to be used for man's responsible self-development and growth as a person, and this is what morality is all about.

What can be read directly in man's physical or biological nature is nothing more than facts (like the law of gravity, etc.), namely how nature works spontaneously. For example, nature causes ovulation to be suspended during the early stages of lactation in a woman who has given birth, and the same effect is produced by taking contraceptive pills. Both of these are facts of nature. The fact that the latter involves man's intelligence and skill to produce the appropriate chemicals in the laboratory does not make it less natural, since the ingredients combine according to the laws of chemistry, and man's creative intelligence is itself part of nature. But 'nature' does not tell us whether it is morally better to make use of one rather than the other of these facts of nature. That one is considered 'artificial' is not sufficient ground for moral condemnation, otherwise tranquilizers and most of the techniques of modern medicine would be immoral. To decide what is morally good, we need an understanding of the meaning and importance of the particular activity or fact of nature in the totality of the human person as such. Thus, which method of birth control is morally right for a couple in the exercise of responsible parenthood will depend on a variety of factors, and not simply on whether it is 'artificial' or not.

Against nature?

A further indication of the weakness of this over-simplified approach to natural law can be found in the variety of practices traditionally condemned as un-natural, therefore against the natural law. Writers of the eastern church (Origen, Clement of Alexandria, Basil) prohibited third and fourth marriages as against natural law. Many of the earlier western writers for-bade even killing in self-defense on the same grounds; it was left to Augustine to define the distinction between justifiable homicide and murder. Clement thought both ear-rings and nose-rings equally for-bidden by the law of nature. Tertullian could not endure the actor's make-up, or the garland of flowers, because they were unnatural, and, as he said, 'ours is a God of nature'. It is easy to smile at these examples from history, but is there not a moral obligation to learn from history? Do we have to wait another cen-tury before asking whether many of the things today condemned as sins against the natural law are really such?

Criticism of the 'blueprint' theory does not mean that there is no such thing as natural law. It is simply to warn against expecting God to communicate his will through a particular channel like the nature of human sexuality, expecting to be able to read off specific precepts of moral law from an examination of man's biological, physiological, psychological or sexual make-up. All that can be read like this in man's nature is the capacity to ethicize, the power to make decisions about right and wrong and to feel bound by them. What those decisions will be in specific areas will depend on a variety of factors, but they are not determined in advance simply by the biological facts.

However, we can speak of a modified version of the 'maker's instructions' theory insofar as we discover basic needs and potentialities in human nature that simply cannot be ignored, and these give us some general insight into values like freedom, responsibility, sociability, love, etc. In striving to promote and preserve these values, experience and reflection will enable us to formulate some general principles like: treat others as you would wish to be treated, some arrangements should be made for the preservation of life, for the regulation of the sex instinct, for the organization of the family and of society. These principles may seem very vague, but they are the basis on which we work out more detailed norms for moral behavior. But the further norms will vary according to changing historical circumstances, both because the same basic value may be served in different ways, and our understanding and appreciation of some values may change. Thus, in a given set of historical circumstances (economic, social, cultural), polygamy might be the best norm for family life, whereas nowadays we look on monogamy as best serving the values of human dignity and family relations.

Absolute norms?

Does this mean that there are no absolute and unchanging moral norms? In fact, it is not very helpful to speak of absolute norms. The expression is confusing insofar as many of the precepts commonly regarded as absolute do actually admit of exceptions. Thus, in spite of the precept: Thou shalt not kill, we justify killing in self-defense and we accept a theology of the just war. Artificial contraception is said to be 'intrinsically evil', i.e. of its very nature wrong, and yet some of the highest authorities accepted that nuns threatened with rape in the Congo could take contraceptive precautions, and many hierarchies say that

married couples may choose whatever method of birth
control their conscience finds best, provided they
avoid abortifacients and whatever would offend the
human dignity of the partners. It was the constant
teaching of theologians that a married couple are
justified in interrupting intercourse if children come
on the scene, but if all forms of contraception except
abstinence during the fertile days are decreed to be
'intrinsically evil', then even this exception is 'against
the natural law', and therefore forbidden by God. The
very phrase 'intrinsically evil' attached to actions like
lying and contraception is a reflection of the old blueprint theory of natural law, with its clearcut, black-
and-white, easily measured moral rules read off from
the physical facts of nature. The phrase immediately
conjures up the notion of an absolute norm, admitting
of no exception. But it is extremely difficult to find
such norms, at least understood in this sense, and
this is the sense most people take to be intended.
Loyalty to the church does not demand that we continue to use a phrase from a bygone age simply because it is consecrated by long usage. Loyalty to God
and to his call that we serve God's people demands
that we cease using terminology that confuses people.
If this phrase needs the involved reasoning of skilled
theologians to explain that it does not really mean what it
says, and at the same time that it nearly does, it were
better dropped altogether. Perhaps it would be going
too far to say that there are no absolute norms, but
they are extremely few. For example, it is almost impossible to envisage circumstances in which the tor-
turing of innocent children would be justified. But
is it really necessary to formulate absolute moral
norms in order to bring home the absoluteness of the
call to be morally good? Rather than speak of absolute
moral norms, it is less confusing and more helpful to

discern the constants in human behavior, the values which provide an overall direction and order in man's development.

The vain search for absolute moral norms is part of the human lust for certainty. It is understandable as part of our moral concern, but not very helpful in striving for moral maturity. The attempt to formulate a long list of them would defeat their purpose by providing a false sense of security. It is true of course that many insights with regard to human conduct have a lasting value and will be passed on from generation to generation, so that we do not have to call everything into question on each occasion. But the norms we formulate are no more than general guidelines, reminders that an important value is at stake. They are not meant to bypass conscience or save us the trouble of thinking. We cannot be satisfied with prefabricated solutions from the past, especially as answers to questions which were never asked in the past. The basic moral call is to grow, to become actually what we are potentially. Insofar as we are continually changing and are faced with new questions, we are called to find new answers. On the basis of experience, inquiry and insight, we must discover which of the various possibilities that present themselves are right, reasonable, human, which of them enable us to grow as persons. It is a flight from personal responsibility to imagine that answers can be found ready-made in scripture or church documents, although we can get valuable insights from these sources. The Second Vatican Council reminds us that the pastors of the church do not always have solutions to every problem which arises, and admits that, in the complicated and rapidly changing world of today, the church needs special help from experts in various sciences in order to 'listen to and distinguish the many

voices of our times, and to interpret them in the light
of the divine Word' (*Church in the Modern World,*
nn. 43-44).

Natural moral law, therefore, is not an external
law or set of precepts to be read off from human nature
and absolutely obeyed. Rather it is an internal law,
functional, dynamic, flexible, not a list of regulations
and commands, but a basic thrust towards self-
determination and fulfillment as a person. It can be
called God's law insofar as he created our human
nature with its fundamental needs, its irrepressible
appetites of heart and mind: for self-preservation,
for endless intellectual inquiry, for social living, for
searching for God. But the best and most human ways
in which these needs are to be met, and therefore the
norms to guide us in meeting them, have not been
spelled out by God. These have to be discovered by
man's experience, inquiry, reflection and decision,
and this is an ongoing process. The moral call is to be
faithful to the demands of each step in this process.

Continual discovery

It is clear from all this that neither in sacred scripture,
nor in the official pronouncements of the church, nor
in what is called natural moral law, can we point to a
set of precepts and say: 'this is God's law' in the
sense of a directly revealed code of morality. This
simple fact ought to alert us to the danger of idolizing
law, allowing it to take the place of God himself. Our
very concern for the sanctity of God and our respect
for his will could well tempt us in that direction, as it
did the pharisees. Our lust for certainty can lure us
along the same path; we would like to know where we

stand before God, how far we can go before getting into the area of sin, etc. But this is not moral maturity.

There is a presumption in favor of law, that it is a good law, that it serves the purpose for which it was formulated and enacted. In general, we trust the legislators in both church and state, and we trust the wisdom and experience of previous generations of Christians, as we accept the laws handed down to us. But obedience to law can never be the whole of morality. To be morally mature is not simply to do what we are told, but to make our own the value which the particular law is intended to protect or promote, and to act from conviction. The real authority of any law, therefore, is not simply the will of the legislator, but the human value at stake (e.g. truthfulness, justice, order in the community, brotherly love). Through passage of time and change of circumstances, laws may cease to serve the value originally intended, in fact even come to defeat their purpose. This is true not only of positive civil law and ecclesiastical legislation, but even of norms claimed to be God's law as revealed in the natural moral law. Such laws lose their authority. Insistence on them creates a credibility gap for leaders. Blind obedience to them stunts moral growth in the individual. Failure to see this is a sinful neglect on the part of the community, a refusal to read the signs of the times as an ongoing revelation of God's call.

It is true to say that sin is a transgression of the law of God in the sense that sin means a refusal to grow into what God wants us to be, a failure to grow into the fullness of the maturity of Christ. But it is an over-simplification to limit sin to the transgression of a law. In Paul's words, law can convict us of sin insofar as it points out to us the areas and sometimes even the ways in which we fail to live up to the Christian ideal. It can spell out the minimum requirements of what God expects of us. But God's call, to the individual and to the whole community, is an ongoing one that cannot be confined to a set of laws, any more than a love relationship between two people can be adequately described by a legal contract. To respond to that call is to grow, but the pattern of our response is something to be continually discovered in the changing circumstances of our lives. It is not enough to examine ourselves in the light of a set of laws and ask how we keep them. It is not enough to ask: what are we doing? We must also ask: what is the doing doing to me? what kind of person am I becoming? Laws can help us to recognize God's call, they can educate our conscience by the insight they give us into human values, but they can never be the full measure of our response, and much less can they ever take the place of the God to whom we respond. In the light of the church's long history of insistence on law and conformity, and its frequent lapses into pharisaism and scribalism, it could do with a healthy dose of relativism. We can still joyfully sing the praises of God's law in psalm 119, provided we preface it and intersperse it with the first of the commandments: 'I am the Lord your God . . . worship no god but me' (Deut 5:6-7).

It should be obvious by now that law is not the absolute that many Christians have taken it to be, though it will always have an essential place in civil society and in the Christian community of the church. What has been said so far should provide the beginnings of an answer to our last question: when is it a sin to break a law? A fuller answer may emerge when we discuss the question of measurement of sin and the ways in which the church should preach morality.

4

HOW FAR CAN I GO?

The first reaction of many traditional Catholics to the question: 'is it a sin?' was to wonder: 'is it allowed?' Not infrequently, this was followed with the query: 'how far can I go?' Law played a dominant role in many people's understanding of morality. This is understandable insofar as laws are an attempt to spell out what the morally good response ought to be in various situations. But it is not easy to put a stop to the spelling out process. People want to know what a law means, to what extent it is binding. Religious authorities thus found themselves obliged to go into the measuring business, with the best intentions and full pastoral concern, but with results that were often less than desirable.

In the old testament the simple precepts of the decalog were teased out until they became the six hundred and thirteen prescriptions observed so punctiliously by the scribes and pharisees. These explained, for example, how far a man might walk on the sabbath without infringing the commandment, and what circumstances might justify him in stretching it. Casuistry, or the art of applying general principles to individual cases, is necessary in order to make morality practicable, but it can also reach a point where it becomes a means for getting around the law. Thus, if the law allowed a journey of a thousand paces from home on the sabbath, one could establish a temporary domicile by placing a pile of one's old clothing at that distance from home on the evening before, and one would then be able to cover twice the normally allowed distance and still observe the letter of the law. In the Catholic tradition, the

lenten fast allowed only one full meal and two colla-
tions or snacks in the day. The relative measure
applied to the latter was that together they should
be less than one full meal, so in order to get full value
from them, one had only to increase the amount of the
main meal.

How much is a sin?

The Council of Trent imposed the serious obligation
of confessing all mortal sins in detail, so the faithful
needed to know exactly when a sin was mortal. For
many people, the question: 'how far may I go before
it is a sin?' was extended to include: 'how far may I
go before it becomes mortal?' With the multiplication
of church laws there was an increasing demand for
theologians and pastors to mark out clearly the
boundaries of sin and the dividing-line between
mortal and venial. One doesn't have to be a cente-
narian to recall the casuistry about Sunday Mass,
fasting, sexuality, to mention only a few areas. A
venial sin was committed by voluntarily missing an
unimportant part of the Mass, e.g. up to the gospel or
after the communion. To miss both of these or the
consecration alone would be mortal. With regard to
the law of fasting, it was common teaching that it
was permitted to interchange the noon and evening
meals, and for a just reason one might also interchange
breakfast and lunch. But to interrupt the principal
meal for more than half an hour without reason would
be a venial sin; should the interruption last more than
an hour it would be mortal. For a proportionately good
reason (e.g. to assist the dying, according to the text-
book) one could interrupt dinner for several hours. As
for the spirit and letter of the fasting law, it was held
that if one had eaten two full meals on a fast day,

either deliberately or by mistake, one could no longer observe the fast and, therefore, might eat as much as he wished afterwards.

A textbook reprinted in the sixties states categorically that 'kissing the private or semi-private parts of the human body is gravely sinful', without any distinction between married or unmarried people. The same manual teaches that it is seriously sinful to look at animals mating, though less serious if it is at a distance or it is a question of small birds. In the matter of justice, the 16th century Scottish theologian, John Major, taught that to steal up to five grains of corn from a rich man's harvest was no sin, from six to ten was a venial sin, and anything more than ten was mortal.

Once involved in the measuring business, it is hard to stop. The original intention and concern were laudable; people need guidelines and directives. But the ultimate consequences in practice could be ridiculous. The idea of adding the tail-end of one Mass to the beginning of another in order to make up the amount specified in the Sunday obligation does not easily fit into our contemporary understanding of eucharistic liturgy. It is not just today or yesterday that people found it hard to believe that a devout, good-living Catholic could be in hell for all eternity for missing one Sunday Mass or eating more than two sausages on Friday. The teaching authorities in the church seemed quite happy to leave people with that impression. But today people will no longer accept that this is the case simply because the church says so. They may be confused in their groping for a more meaningful understanding of sin, but they are very conscious of the shortcomings of the older approach, and are particularly unhappy at the consequences of some of the older teaching.

Legalism and complacency

Over-emphasis on law measurement can lead to legalism, minimalism, complacency and scrupulosity. We recall Jesus' condemnation of the scribes and pharisees for their exaggerated reverence for the law and their minute measuring of it, and we know that the Christian community has not always escaped the same temptation. A new insight, a new discovery in Christian experience can be robbed of its vitality when legalism takes over, when it is frozen into a law and rigidly imposed. It has often been remarked that the worst thing that could happen to the documents of the Second Vatican Council would be to transform them into a new code of canon law. Minimalism is to be found in people who feel that there is no sin where a matter is not covered by law or cannot be easily measured. This explains why so many people confess to missing part of Mass or eating meat on a day of abstinence, but seem oblivious to the possibility of sin in their insensitivity to their married partner, their lack of concern for the underprivileged, or their share in the atmosphere of prejudice and discrimination in their community or work situation. Basic attitudes are not easily measured or legislated for, so they were frequently forgotten in an examination of conscience. With so much emphasis on identifiable and measurable sins, less attention was paid to general sinfulness, either in the individual person or in the community as a whole.

Complacency and harsh judgment of others are always a danger for the law-abiding citizen and the conscientious Christian, but the danger is increased when fidelity is measured in terms of precise law, and morality is seen more in terms of quantity than quality. When morality is spelled out in so many laws, it is as though each law earned a certain number of marks, like questions in an examination, so that one's total of credits could be banked to one's account in heaven. With this attitude, it is easy to give the impression that one can score full marks, that one may go before God with an easy conscience and claim one's reward. Jesus had little time for this attitude, and in his story of the pharisee and the publican he made it clear that quantity counts for little. Measuring one's own goodness by the yardstick of law, it is difficult to avoid the temptation to measure the failures of others by the same law and take comfort from the contrast. But the goodness preached by Jesus is not measurable in terms of quantity at all. What he looks for is the quality of our conduct, that it reproduce something of his own basic attitude, in Paul's words, that we 'have that mind which was in Christ Jesus.' This may be present in actions that, objectively speaking, hardly seem virtuous at all, as in the case of many neurotics, and be almost totally absent in the acts of politeness that are merely the result of good breeding and expensive education. Only God can judge where each one of us stands in his sight. Since he alone is good, and our own goodness is his gift to us, none of us can afford to be complacent or presume to judge our neighbors because they don't measure up to our standard.

Scrupulosity

If Jesus had little time for the complacent, he would surely be very sympathetic to the scrupulous. There are good, conscientious people afflicted with this psychological problem, and our multiplicity of laws and concern for measurement provides a fertile field for them to indulge their weakness and intensify their suffering. A Roman psychiatrist with an international

clientele once remarked that of all his patients suffering from this problem, only Roman Catholics had
religious scruples. No matter how much advice and
counselling they are given, they still agonize over
whether a particular thought, word or deed was a sin,
and whether it was mortal or venial. Added to the
ordinary pain of indecision and compulsive worry,
there is the awful fear of eternal punishment in the
background. If such people did not have a religious
upbringing which laid such emphasis on law and the
precise measurement of sin, there is no guarantee that
they would be free of the psychological disturbance
of scruples, but at least their problem would not
be aggravated.

Emphasis on precise measurement in the assessment of sin came to some extent from the church's
experience of the sacrament of penance. Not only did
the faithful have the obligation to confess all serious
sins according to number and kind, but the confessor
was obliged to see that they did. The Roman Ritual,
in its instructions on this sacrament, stressed the role
of the confessor as physician and judge. The moral
theologians spelled out more particularly the latter
function. A text-book widely used in the sixties puts
it: 'As judge, the confessor must pass judgment on the
penitent before absolving him, and for this reason it
is sometimes necessary to ask questions. In passing
judgment the priest must consider both the sins and
the disposition of the penitent. Sins are judged according to their quantity and quality. The duty to ask
questions, to insure the integrity of the confession,
is grave.' While most confessors were sympathetic
and fatherly in dealing with penitents, some, through
a scrupulous sense of responsibility or impelled by
other subconscious motivation, applied a kind of
third degree questioning that reinforced people's
concern with measurement. For some, the sacrament

was almost a court of law in which the priest was like a public attorney looking for an exact reconstruction of the crime, a judge trying to establish the precise degree of culpability, so that every last ounce of guilt could be accounted for. The new rites for this sacrament of reconciliation show a very different emphasis.

The 'sin-grid'

It would be unfair to paint a caricature, but if people are to be helped to a more mature understanding of morality and sin, it is necessary to acknowledge the weakness of the over-simplified older approach. It had the merit of being clear, easily taught, easily measured, easily supervised — at least in appearance. But a price had to be paid for this false clarity and unexamined security. Casuistry tended to isolate the individual sin from the overall behavior of the penitent. Fidelity to God was split up into detailed, individual actions, taking attention away from the sinfulness of basic attitudes, trends and dispositions. The 'sin-grid' for examination of conscience established lists of sins individually registered and catalogued, with their varying degrees of seriousness: mortal and venial, sins of weakness and sins of malice. Not only was there an individualistic approach to sins in the life of an individual person, but this carried over into an individualistic approach to the individual sinner apart from the community. In spite of the doctrine of the Mystical Body of Christ, little attention was paid to the darker side of the coin, to our solidarity in sin, to the sinfulness of a whole community. In the area of confession, it was easy to think that we could pay our fine, make restitution, merit forgiveness, and forget that God's pardon is always pure gift, not a reward that can be earned.

It would be a mistake of course, to conclude from all
this that a Christian must be antinomian, that we can
do without laws, that we have no need to spell out the
meaning of sin, or that we can ignore the fact of degrees
of seriousness in sin. It is true that the law of Christ
is a law of love, but it is an over-simplification leading
to moral laxity to claim that love is our only criterion.
St. Paul could preach liberty from law, but at the
same time felt it necessary to point to specific behavior that contradicted the new life in the Spirit.
He told the Galatians: 'If the Spirit leads you, then
you are not subject to the law. What human nature
does is quite plain. It shows itself in immoral, filthy,
and indecent actions; in worship of idols and witch-
craft. People become enemies and they fight; they
become jealous, angry, and ambitious. They separate
into parties and groups; they are envious, get drunk,
have orgies, and do other things like these. I warn
you now as I have before: those who do these things
will not possess the kingdom of God' (5:18-21).

Identifying sin

Both in old and new testaments, the people of God
needed practical directives to identify sinful activities
and were aware that there was a gradation of gravity
in sin. It was recognized that Israel's sins were more
serious than those of others because of the special
privilege and intimacy of their covenant relationship
with God, and those of the Christian community were
considered still more serious (Heb 10:26-31). The old
testament has several catalogues of sins (Deut 27:15-
26; Amos 2:4-8; 8:4-6; Hos 4:2; Ezek 18:5-20). Jesus
himself gives an abbreviated version of the decalog
list in answer to the rich young man's question about
the conditions for receiving eternal life (Mk 10:18-19),
and gives further examples of sinful behavior in his

description of the last judgment (Mt 25:41-46). There are several lists of vices and sins in the rest of the new testament (I Cor 6:9-10; Gal 5:19-21; Rom 1:24-32; 13:1-14; I Tim 1:4-11; I Pet 4:2-5; 2 Pet 2:12-22).

In the light of this experience, there can be no question of the Christian community at any stage dispensing with such practical guidelines, though we need to remember that some of the scriptural lists are culturally conditioned and therefore require some care when applied to modern times. For example, when Paul spoke of homosexuals in Rom 1:26-27 or I Cor 6:9, he could not have been aware of the fact that a large percentage of the population are not personally responsible for their homosexual orientation. Likewise, it would be an abuse of scripture to quote his lists and catalogues of mortal sins, and especially to claim that each and every act, on Paul's authority, is a mortal sin. Our notion of mortal sin, with the obligation of confession, was simply unknown to Paul. But Augustine held him to mean that one does not need to have all these vices to be excluded from the kingdom of heaven; any one alone would suffice, and each and every act of these vices is a mortal sin. He went on to teach that in lists like this we have God telling us precisely which sins are mortal. He admits that, without such revelation, we might be tempted to judge some of these sins much more lightly. He recalls that hellfire is threatened on the man who merely calls his brother a fool. Augustine the bishop and pastor was concerned to make people aware of the seriousness of sin and the need for penance, but there seems to have been nobody in his congregation to ask him if he wasn't over-simplifying with his hard-sell.

The people of God have always been conscious of degrees of seriousness in sin, but the gradation was differently understood at different times. Our modern

notion of mortal sin is not to be found as such in scripture or the early church, since it is so much conditioned by the church's legislation about confession,
which is of much later origin. The clearest text to
speak of degrees in sin is St. John's first letter: 'If you
see your brother commit a sin that does not lead to
death, you should pray to God, who will give him life.
This applies to those whose sins do not lead to death.
But there is sin which leads to death, and I do not say
that you should pray to God about that. All wrongdoing is sin, but there is sin which does not lead to
death' (5:16-17). It is clear that, for John, not all sins
are on the same level, that some are more serious than
others. It is not clear what precisely is the sin that
leads to death, or the 'deadly sin'. In the context, it
probably refers to the 'sin against the Holy Spirit',
final impenitence, the attitude of the person who
simply refuses forgiveness and is impervious to the
power of prayer (Mt 12:31-32; Mk 3:28-30; Lk 12:10).

Basic attitude

This reference to 'attitude' recalls an important element in the biblical notion of sin. Though it it clear
in both old and new testaments that individual actions
can be sinful, the emphasis is more on sin as a basic
attitude, a state of sinfulness. In his various catalogues, Paul was not so much listing sins as describing
the kind of people who exclude themselves from the
kingdom of heaven by their way of life. He also speaks
of the 'slavery of sin, which leads to death' (Rom 6:16).
The sinful attitude, of course, is built up by individual
actions, as James writes: 'A person is tempted when
he is drawn away and trapped by his own evil desire.
Then his evil desire conceives and gives birth to sin;
and sin, when it is full-grown, gives birth to death'
(1:14-15). John too speaks more of sin as a state than

of individual sinful actions. To emphasize the seriousness of the sinful state he quotes Jesus at the last
supper: 'Whoever hates me hates my Father also. They
would not be guilty of sin if I had not done among them
the things that no one else ever did; as it is, they have
seen what I did, and they hate both me and my Father'
(Jn 15:23-24). Sin is a continuing state of hatred of
God, and contrasted with new life in the Spirit it is
death. 'We know that we have left death and come over
into life; we know it because we love our brothers.
Whoever does not love is still under the power of
death' (I Jn 3:14). This is the origin of our notion
of mortal sin or sinfulness, namely a state of mind
and will, a way of life amounting to a total rejection
of God, a condition of total selfishness. Nowhere in the
new testament do we get a list of individual mortal
sins meriting the punishment of hell or needing confession and special absolution, but the various sin-
lists are warnings and indications as to the kind of
behavior that can lead to the state of mortal sinfulness,
spiritual death.

The early Christians soon discovered that in spite
of their new life in Christ, they were still subject to
temptation and sin, so there was need for repentance
and continual conversion, hence the warnings of the
sin-lists. But Paul was no believer in do-it-yourself
sanctity. The community is a central theme in his
theology, and he was particularly conscious of the
harm that could be done to the community by the
presence of an unrepentant sinner. We see the beginnings of the practice of excommunication in I Cor
5:3-11. The sinner was to be excluded from the community and shunned by his fellow-believers, both
to shock him into repentance and to protect the community from the contagion of his sinfulness. This
practice came to be systematized by later generations
in the church, which imposed canonical penance as a

condition for the re-admission of those excommunicated, and specified the sins which merited the
penalty of excommunication. These were called
'crimes, grave sins, capital sins'. The main ones were
idolatry, apostasy, murder, abortion and publicly-
known adulterous relationship. They were 'grave'
not so much because of the degree of personal guilt,
but rather because they caused scandal and serious
injury to the church. For centuries the sinner could
be re-admitted only once in a lifetime, but gradually
re-admission became more frequent and the list of
'grave sins' became more extensive, including even
internal sins. The Celtic missionaries who were
responsible for the development of frequent confession drew up a sliding scale of penances for the various
sins, and soon the church was fully involved in the
measuring business. These tariffed penances were
proportioned to the external act, without any reference to the degree of moral responsibility. The final
phase came when the Council of Trent decreed that
penitents were to confess all mortal sins according
to number and kind.

Mortal and venial

The decree did not specify what constituted mortal
sin, so it was left to moral theologians and canonists
to answer the questions of the faithful on the point.
Mortal sin came to be defined as the transgression
of a divine law in a grievous matter with full knowledge and full consent. The text-books distinguished:
1) Sins which according to their nature could never
be venial, allowing of no lightness of matter (e.g.
unbelief, lewd desires). Such sins could be venial
only through imperfect attention or partial consent.
2) Sins whose matter is important in itself, but which
in particular cases may be light; thus theft may be

mortal or venial depending on the amount stolen.
3) Sins that always remain venial as long as no circumstances is superadded to change the nature of the
sin, e.g. immoderation in sleep or laughter, although
these may become mortal sins because of an erroneous
conscience. Venial sin in general is when the matter
is light or there is not full knowledge or consent.
The textbooks also contained elaborate criteria for
measuring not only the gravity, but also the number
and kind of sins. Furthermore, since laws were binding in conscience, people wanted to know of individual laws whether they obliged under pain of mortal
or venial sin, and for laws that could be quantitatively
measured they wanted to know what quantity of time
or matter was required for mortal sin. Hence the 'sin-
grid' familiar to generations of Catholics, the long list
of sins with their ascending or descending degrees of
gravity, and their aggravating or extenuating
circumstances.

Since the 'matter' of these sins was clearly cate-
gorized as mortal or venial, there was little room for
discussion. The burden of the enquiry then shifted
to the degree of awareness or the amount of consent
in order to establish the gravity of the sin. This was
the area in which the confessor sometimes asked: 'did
you take pleasure in it?' Since, in many cases, the
examination was done long after the event, which
may have been quite hazy in the first instance, it was
not always possible to come up with a clear verdict,
so for the sake of safety, the phrase 'insofar as God
sees me guilty' was added to the confession of such
sins.

Since mortal sin was considered to mean the rejection of God by the fully deliberate refusal to obey
him in one of his commandments, it involved the loss
of sanctifying grace, the divine life in the soul. This
meant spiritual death, and a person dying in that state

would be punished by an eternity in hell. It was a very serious affair, determining one's destiny in the after-life, and the fear it engendered often gave rise to con-siderable scrupulosity. On the other hand, a certain laxity developed towards sins which were dismissed as 'only venial'.

False clarity

It is true that this simple, clearcut approach helped many people to examine their conscience truthfully and make sincere and fruitful confessions. The cas-uistry of moral theologians was a genuine pastoral concern to mix mercy and justice, to find a reasonable solution in the apparent conflict between inflexible principle and the intractable human situation. But the clarity and simplicity are only apparent. Today's Catholics no longer accept such a simple rule of thumb. Modern psychology has added several nuances to the notion of 'full knowledge and full consent', and we have come to realize that isolated actions, bits of behavior, cannot be given moral labels unless under-stood in terms of their human meaning, and this is not possible except in the context of the total person-ality. The great theologians like Aquinas and Bona-venture were careful to explain that in listing actions that were matter for mortal sin, they were simply providing an extrinsic criterion, a general indication of the kind of action that would normally involve a person's basic moral stance and require a choice that would be fundamentally for God or self. But the later tradition, concerned with measurement and control, came to attribute an independent and almost absolute value to the external action. In the minds of the vast majority of the faithful, to miss Sunday Mass deliber-ately without justification was a mortal sin and to die before repenting of it meant eternity in hell. Perhaps some of the clergy might have been able to explain that the position was never quite as harsh as that, but they seldom told the faithful.

Fundamental option

St. Paul, the old testament prophets, and most of all Jesus himself continually stressed that true religion was a matter of the heart, not simply as the symbolic seat of the emotions, but as the core of the whole personality. All of the commandments are simply expressions of the basic command to 'love God with all your heart, with all your soul, and with all your mind, and love your neighbor as yourself' (Mt 22:37-39). This involves first and foremost a basic choice about what is supremely important in life, a fundamental attitude or stance that will be expressed in our thoughts, words and deeds. Deep in our hearts we take a stand on the way we intend to live our life; for God and others, or totally for self, symbolized by Mammon or the idols of the world, such as money, power, ambition. God calls us to choose. We cannot live with a divided heart. As Jesus puts it: 'You cannot serve both God and money' (Mt 6:24). The explicit choice for God may be made in a peak moment of religious experience and further renewed in prayer and action, or it may simply take shape as the overall pattern of our lives built up by, and expressed in, the individual decisions of daily living. On the other hand, mortal sin, in the biblical sense, is to choose self before God, to make something other than God the center of one's life. This may be done in a single moment, when a clear decision is made involving one's subsequent life, or, more frequently, it may be the result of a slow process of moral and spiritual decline.

Theologians today speak of this as our *basic choice,* or *fundamental option,* our general *life-direction,* for or against God. This basic attitude of will flows from the core of our personality and determines the overall pattern of our lives. But not all our decisions and actions are central in the sense of coming from the center of our person. Many of our actions are at the periphery and not at the center. They come from instinctual drives, both positive and negative, such as the sexual urge, aggressiveness, fear, insecurity, all of which obscure our insight, or from routine, so that our full freedom is not involved. Such actions may be in line with our basic option, perhaps strengthening it, or they may be inconsistent with it and so weaken it, though not central enough to change it. It is clear that mortal sinfulness in the biblical sense of spiritual death is not present unless in the case of central acts coming from the core of our personality, acts which change our basic attitude away from God. The change need not be a dramatic one concentrated in a single act, but we can discover that we have arrived at such a state where God has been excluded from our lives. Human life, however, is seldom a clearcut, black-and-white picture, and the human heart has its own deviousness and perversity, so we cannot be certain where we stand in God's eyes. Only God himself knows. 'I, the Lord, search the minds and test the hearts of men. I treat each one according to the way he lives, according to what he does' (Jer 17:10). Thomas Aquinas reminds us that we can never have more than a moral certainty that we are in the state of grace. Hence, though we trust in the infinite love and mercy of God who is our Father, we work out our salvation in fear and trembling.

Living with uncertainty

Christian realism demands that we accept this uncertainty and learn to live with it. This applies not only to our basic option, but even to individual sin-actions. Such is the basic imperfection of our human nature, the influence of subconscious factors, the weight of external pressures from the sinful world around us, and the gradual and groping development of our freedom and moral insight, that we can seldom be sure that a particular action is central, that it flows from the core of our personality and the depth of our conscience. Here too we must beware of the lust for certainty. It is far more helpful to keep our eyes firmly fixed on Jesus our model and the ideals he sets before us than to become preoccupied with self by trying to gauge the precise measure of our failure or virtue. It does not follow, however, that the external action is of little account, that we have nothing to learn from the sin-lists of scripture or church documents. The community, in the light of its experience of human nature, intends such lists to indicate that certain actions are so serious in their consequences that a morally developed person performing them could normally presume that they came from the center of his person and not from the periphery. He could well have a moral certainty that such is the case, but no one else is ever justified in pointing a finger at him and judging that he is in mortal sin.

No matter how fickle or inconsistent people may be, however, there is a basic continuity in human living, so that one does not change one's fundamental option every second day. Psychologically, it simply does not make sense to think of people swinging in and out of mortal sin every Friday and Saturday. This ought to alert us to the inadequacy of our traditional mortal-venial division of sin. Mortal sin as presented in our traditional catechisms cannot be simply equated with the mortal sinfulness which is spiritual death described in the biblical texts. The bible distinguishes between sins that amount to a rejection of God, hence spiritual death, and lesser sins, the result of human weakness or inattention, the sins into which even the just man falls seven times a day. Modern psychology distinguishes between basic option and the actions that flow from the center of the person, on the one hand, and peripheral actions on the other, actions that do not engage the totality of the person. But the traditional mortal-venial distinction of the catechism owes its origin to the church's discipline for the sacrament of confession. Mortal sins, in this tradition, are those for which sacramental confession is required before communion. Because they obviously included the biblical kind of mortal sinfulness, and the same name 'mortal' was used, all sins subsequently listed as 'mortal' were understood in the biblical sense, and confusion followed.

Threefold division

Theologians today prefer a threefold division: 1) mortal sinfulness, 2) serious or grave sin, and 3) less serious or venial sin, in general the daily faults of the earnest good man. The term 'mortal sinfulness' is used in the biblical sense explained above. Some of the 'mortal sins' of the catechism tradition could well come within this category, if they involve a change of basic option. Others would not. For example, the decision to omit Sunday Mass, for one person, might well be the final step and the external expression of a state of mind that had already become alienated from God. The same decision, for another person, might be nothing more than laziness or a bout of depression, leaving intact his basic orientation towards God. The new category 'serious or grave sin' would straddle the old mortal-venial division, insofar as some sins once considered 'mortal' do not involve total alienation from God (and so do not merit the title 'mortal sinfulness'), and on the other hand, some of those formerly considered 'venial' cannot be simply dismissed as 'only venial'.

The older tradition, at least in its popular understanding, had a clear boundary-line for mortal sin, and everything short of that was considered venial. But there is a world of difference between the ordinary daily sins of weakness, the occasional delays, halts and even minor detours of the man sincerely trying to walk in the path of the Lord, and the creeping paralysis, the emptiness of the one who pays lip-service to God, but doesn't really *care*, who blinds himself to his growing alienation from God with the rationalization that his sins are 'only venial'. In the light of what we have said about central and peripheral acts, the good man sincerely doing his best need not worry even if he experiences serious defects. His 'heart' is in the right place. He knows that he cannot rely on his own strength, but all his trust is in the Lord, and he makes his conversion a daily-renewed life-commitment.

Perhaps at this point the old lust for certainty will again make its appearance. People will accept this new threefold division, but immediately ask for a list of sins for each category. It would be a mistaken kindness on the part of theologians or pastors to meet the request. There is real need for a catechesis of sin, but a new 'sin-grid' to replace the old would be disastrous. Surely the time has come to trust people to grow up, to take the emphasis off measurement and control. The old sin-lists can still be referred to, even developed to encompass new problems and situations, but without the mortal-venial labels that encourage a quantitative approach to morality, with all its dangers of legalism, minimalism, complacency and scrupulosity. A later chapter will deal with the problem of 'teaching morality', for parents, teachers, pastors, in fact for all the teaching authorities in the church, but a few points may be appropriate in the present context. The real challenge is to enable people to internalize and make their own the basic Christian values, to evaluate their daily living in the light of these values, and to go on forming their conscience in an ever-growing sensitivity to what God expects. Morality cannot simply be decreed. People need to be persuaded and convinced, so it is not enough to label something a 'sin' or a 'mortal sin' and leave it at that.

Objective sin?

The first step in meeting this challenge is to avoid using language that is ambiguous and confusing. To describe something as 'objectively sinful', implying that it is sinful in itself, though it might be without subjective guilt owing to lack of knowledge or full freedom, is not helpful to people who want to know what sin is. There are no 'objective sins'. Sin is present only where the person freely chooses something which he personally knows to be evil. His action may be bad or wrong or evil in the sense that it is harmful to others or to himself, and so may be described objectively as 'wrongdoing', but it is not a *moral* evil, not a 'sin', unless he himself judges it to be wrong and yet goes ahead and does it. However, even though an individual may not be subjectively guilty of sin in a particular action, he is responsible for the consequences of it, and so may be bound to make 'restitution' for the harm he caused.

The word 'sin' cannot be applied to a physical activity as such, but only to the total action in its human meaning, therefore including motive and circumstances. In fact, the same physical activity can have several human meanings. Thus, killing may be murder, self-defense or carrying out a legally-decreed death-sentence. Speaking a falsehood may be lying or preserving a secret to save a life. An act of human intercourse might be an expression of married love, rape (even within marriage), hatred of women, etc. These are essentially different human actions, not the same action plus different motives or circumstances. It is only the total act, with its full human meaning for the person doing it, that can be described as 'sin'. This does not mean that the physical component does not enter into the moral assessment of a particular action. Normally, the physical action is an expression of the doer's attitude of will, so that, for example, it is generally presumed that one who deliberately burns down his neighbor's house has more hatred than one who merely calls him names. But the physical act alone cannot decide the sinfulness of the action.

Intrinsic evil?

If one should speak of 'objective wrongdoing' rather than 'objective sin', the same caution applies to the use of the word 'evil' and particularly the phrase 'intrinsically evil'. An evil is a disvalue, something harmful to man, like poverty, suffering, disease, injury, death. Whatever good consequences they may occasionally have, these are bad or evil in themselves. We have a moral obligation to fight them as far as possible. But they are not sins, not *moral* evils, whether they are caused by chance, by natural causes or by human action. Even when caused by human action, in themselves they still remain *non-moral* or *pre-moral* evils. The word *moral* attaches only to free human behavior. These pre-moral evils do not become moral evils until they are willed for their own sake, without proportionate reason. In this case, they still remain pre-moral evils in themselves, bad things to happen, but they are *moral* evils, immoral actions, sins, only for the persons bringing them

about, e.g. inflicting injury or death without proportionate reason. Thus, to kill a man with no justi-
fying reason is a sin, a moral as well as a pre-moral
or non-moral evil. Killing a man in self-defense is
still evil, a pre-moral evil, a bad thing to happen,
something to regret and to be done only with great
reluctance, but it is *not morally evil* or *sinful,* it is
part of the morally good act of self-defense. Too often
in the past we marched off to battle and killed with
gusto because we reasoned that the war was just.
It was too easily forgotten that the killing was still
evil, a bad thing to have to do, even though it might
not be counted as sin.

To say that something is 'intrinsically evil' means
that it is evil of its very nature, and the impression
is given that nothing would ever justify it. We can say
of non-moral or pre-moral evils like death, injury,
sickness, etc. that they are evil in themselves, and in
that sense intrinsically evil. But it does not follow
that there are never situations in which they are
necessary and therefore justified. It serves no purpose to use the phrase 'intrinsically evil' of pre-moral
evils, especially since it gives rise to such confusion.

It makes even less sense to apply it to *moral evils,*
or sins, since these are always individual human
actions each with its own motive and circumstances. The same physical action, e.g. using contraceptives, for one person may be an exercise in responsible married love and parenthood, and for his
neighbor an act of selfishness. To say that artificial
methods of contraception are intrinsically evil is to
give the impression that in no circumstances could
they be morally justified. But this is not the case.
They are said to be immoral as a means of responsible
parenthood, yet it is commonly admitted that nuns
threatened with rape may take contraceptive precautions, and that contraceptive pills may be taken

for therapeutic reasons (regularize the cycle, etc). All three cases involve the same pills, working in the same way according to God's chemical and physiological laws. Since the main difference is the intention or motive, it cannot be the 'artificial contraception' which is evil, but the whole human action involving motive and circumstances, in which case 'intrinsically evil' makes little sense, since we are then talking about an individual action and not a whole class of actions.

Theologians nowadays generally admit that the phrase 'intrinsically evil' as applied to moral evil makes no logical sense and cannot be defended logically. Perhaps out of reverence for traditional usage, some try to justify it on the basis of pastoral concern for formulating practical norms. It is claimed that if questioning were allowed in some cases, exceptions would multiply, hence the need for a simple direct prohibition. This seems a short-sighted pastoral policy. The church may be concerned about psychological and sociological as well as logical factors when formulating moral norms, but pastors who ignore logic too blatantly are insulting the God-given intelligence of the faithful and putting a premium on a kind of unquestioning simplicity which does not help moral maturity or responsibility. That the phrase could profitably be dropped is shown by the fact that the Holy See's *Declaration on Abortion* (1974) makes no use of it whatever and yet presents a very convincing moral argument, whereas the *Declaration on Sexual Ethics* (1975) uses it freely with reference to masturbation and homosexuality and signally fails to prove its point.

Under pain of sin?

Another phrase that might well be dropped in the church is that certain laws are binding 'under pain of

mortal sin'. From all that has been said above, it
should be clear that the transgression of no law can
automatically be described as mortal sin. Neither
the authority making the law nor a lawyer commen-
tator nor a moral theologian can specify the precise
moral obligation of a particular law. This will depend
on the individual, the situation, and particularly the
value the particular law has in promoting the welfare
of the individual or the community. A law that is
arbitrary simply cannot bind in conscience. The individual needs to be aware of his own limitations and
bias, and realize the wisdom of the old saying that
no one is a judge in his own case, but a law will appeal
to his conscience only to the extent that he is convinced of its necessity or usefulness. It is true that
the code of canon law decrees that 'laws made to
counter a common danger impose an obligation even
though this danger does not exist in the particular
case' (canon 21), but a much older tradition left more
to conscience by the principle that a law founded on
presumption of common danger loses its binding force
when the presumption is not verified. All laws are
binding in conscience, but the extent of the obligation
is not something that can be precisely measured and
expressed in a blanket phrase applicable to all.

Most clearly of all, no lawgiver has the power to
impose the sanction of mortal sin, and certainly not
eternal punishment. To decree that 'dancing after
midnight or attendance at non-Catholic schools is
a mortal sin' is simply nonsense. If the situation
demands it, a legal sanction may be applied (e.g. the
lawbreaker may be excommunicated or denied certain privileges), but the legal order should not be
confused with the moral. The two orders simply do
not coincide. An individual who has been excommunicated loses his standing in the community, but
it does not necessarily follow that he has lost his

standing with God. No one can deprive him of divine grace and his relationship with God. If the relationship is strained or broken, he alone is responsible, because God is the ever-faithful, infinite lover who never goes back on his word.

Divine paradox

The question: 'how far can I go before it is a mortal sin?' is too much like the attitude of a husband who would ask his wife: 'how much can I play around before you consider me definitely unfaithful?' or: 'how far can I stretch our relationship before it breaks?' A more Christian attitude is: 'how much can I give? how much can I love? how do I show my love?' Our conversion and commitment to the Lord must be continually renewed, and from time to time we need to look into our hearts and take stock of our position. But in evaluating our response to God, whether positive or negative, we should not look for more clarity and security than is possible. A relationship cannot be measured in quantitative terms. It is the quality that counts. Of course, the quality is shown in action, as Jesus makes clear in his description of the final judgment (Mt 25:31-46), but the quality itself is not subject to material measurement. We need to beware of false security and the lust for certainty. The spiritual tension we experience can be a healthy safeguard against the dangers that flow from over-concern with measurement, and it is something we must learn to live with. It should certainly warn us against judging by appearances and measurable results. The divine quality that God expects to see reflected in our action may be present even at very lowly levels of achievement. The neurotic or psychologically crippled person may be very close to God although the expression of his love is hindered and blocked by disabilities for which he is not responsible. On the other hand, the divine quality flowing from 'that mind which was in Christ Jesus' is never fully present even in the activity of the saint, because only God himself is totally good. There must be millions of saints far higher in heaven than the ones we have been able to measure and canonize. God's ways are not our ways, and Jesus himself warns against the dangers of measurement with his paradox about the first being last, the last being first, and the weak confounding the strong.

5

HOW SINFUL IS SEX?

One of the reasons for confusion about the notion of sin today is our preoccupation with sexuality. The saddest commentary on the church's moral teaching is that when a person is described as immoral, most people think of sexual sin. The individual may be selfish, greedy, spiteful, cruel, jealous, unjust, brutal, violent, unscrupulous, arrogant, but he will not be thought immoral unless he is involved in sexual sin. Not only did traditional moral teaching seem to pay more attention to the sixth and ninth commandments than to the others, but its understanding of sex was predominantly negative. There seemed little in the sexual sphere that was not sinful. Any positive treatment of the subject spiritualized it to the extent of almost losing contact with the world of reality. The bulk of the teaching was concerned with the danger of sex, and the textbooks were even hesitant about what was 'permitted' to engaged couples and married people. It is not sufficiently realized how much of this attitude is owed to non-Christian influences in the early centuries and failure to benefit from the insights and discoveries of the human sciences. Sin is as much a reality in the sexual area as in any other, but if we are to get a balanced understanding of it we need to look critically at the factors that influenced our tradition and see how we can make the Christian view of sex meaningful in today's world.

Sexual wilderness

A reaction against the over-emphasis and negative treatment of the past is the tendency among many

priests and teachers to soft-pedal it now, to take it
for granted that the subject has too many gray areas
to allow us to speak clearly of sin. There is a real risk
in this, insofar as a generation of teenagers are growing up without any norms or guidelines in this most
difficult area of their development, and what we are
witnessing is not so much a sexual revolution as
simply a sexual wilderness. This in turn provokes a
reaction from those who complain bitterly about
the 'permissiveness' of the age and want pastors to
preach the old black-and-white rules, conveniently
forgetting that many of those who swing along with
the so-called permissiveness were themselves brought
up on such rules.

It is sad to see such polarization in the church. But
in reacting against these two extremes and searching
for a positive and meaningful view of sex in the context of Christian faith, we need to beware of a certain
'mystique' of sex, the kind of glorification of sexual
activity embodied in the view that 'bad sex is better
than no sex'. It is no exaggeration to say that our
western culture is obsessed with sex, and we need
to be reminded that obsession with sexuality is every
bit as inhuman as suppression of sexuality. Our concern for a new and more meaningful understanding
of it should be seen, not as a last-minute rush to catch
up with the 'modern world', but rather in the context
of our attempt to understand the sexual dimension of
our human nature in the service of love.

That the sexual dimension is no minor matter is
recognized in the opening paragraph of the Holy See's
Declaration on Sexual Ethics (1975), which says: 'The
human person, present-day scientists maintain, is so
profoundly affected by sexuality that it must be considered one of the principal formative influences on
the life of a man or woman. In fact, sex is the source

of the biological, psychological and spiritual characteristics which make a person male or female and
which thus considerably influence each individual's
progress towards maturity and membership of society.' This simple statement has implications for
Christian morality that were seldom recognized in
the older tradition. But the older tradition has so
molded, not only our thinking, but more so our feeling
and gut-level reactions, that it is difficult for many
people to adjust to the new insights. As in the previous
chapters, it is necessary to take a critical look at the
older tradition and explicitly recognize its shortcomings in order to exorcise the ghosts that haunt
our imagination. Again it could be objected that it is
not fair to criticize the past, and it is so easy to paint
a caricature. But the fact remains that much of our
thinking is still subconsciously affected by factors
seldom explicitly adverted to. To face these explicitly
and recognize their influence will help to clarify our
thinking.

The positive strand

It would be totally untrue to say that the older tradition had no positive and healthy teaching on sexuality
and Christian chastity. One can find the basis for such
teaching in the bible itself, beginning with Genesis.
The bible 'demythologized' sex, took it out of the realm
of the gods, with its fertility rites and temple prosti-
tution, and made it something basically human and
good. The creation narrative is quite explicit: 'God
made human beings, male and female . . . and God was
pleased with what he saw. The man and woman were
both naked, but they were not embarrassed' (Gen 1-2).
The Song of Songs describes the physical beauty and
erotic love of two young people, a relationship that

is sensuous, passionate, fully human. The prophets, and later St. Paul, were not ashamed to use the marital relationship as a metaphor for God's love for his people. The gospels make no mention of Jesus ever giving genital expression to his sexuality, but Hebrews tells us that he was like us in all things but sin. He was a sexual being, and the affective dimension of his personality is clear from the picture we have of him as a compassionate, gentle, loving, tender and warm person who touched people physically, psychologically and spiritually.

The positive strand in our tradition was never lost down through the centuries, and in every age there were people whose common sense, emotional balance and secure family background enabled them to appreciate and live it. They were not unduly perturbed by the more negative strands in the tradition, and they are the people who today are best able to understand and appropriate the new insights from the human sciences because they have already been discovering them implicitly in their own experience. This fact needs not merely to be tacitly admitted, but in the interests of truth and justice to be loudly proclaimed. Any new sexual ethic must be in continuity with the best of the past, although the deeper continuity may sometimes involve a radical discontinuity at certain points. But the best of the past was far from being the whole of the past. Even a slight acquaintance with marriage counselling, confessional practice and the history of moral theology should make it clear that for large numbers of people the positive strand was a remote ideal, only hazily glimpsed through a dark fog of emotional hang-ups, religious scruples and guilt. Knowledge alone is not virtue, but a sober look at some of the ingredients in that fog may help to clear away the mist from such people's minds and enable them not merely to cope with their sexuality, but to rejoice in it as God's gift.

Moralism

One of the reasons for today's confusion is moralism, the temptation on the part of pastors, parents and teachers to teach morality by decree. When society was less democratic and there was more unquestioning acceptance of authority, preachment and prescription served well enough. But from their first years in school, children are now taught to question and discover things for themselves, and they cannot understand why religion should be an exception. As young adults they find that their questions about the Christian meaning of sexuality are not getting convincing answers. Some of the answers remind them of the preacher's sermon notes with the red-pencilled directive in the margin: 'argument weak here, shout like hell!' It is false loyalty to the church to pretend that our argument was never weak, that we were never ignorant of the facts, that we never overstated the case.

History is there to show how much the church's teaching has changed through the centuries. A narrow view of the church's teaching role has given the impression that the changes were only minor details, and that on all major points there is an unbroken line of tradition going back to scripture itself or to the early Christian communities. This is simply not the case. It is too easily forgotten that it was the constant teaching for centuries that intercourse had to be for the purpose of procreation in order to be free of sin, that intercourse during menstruation or pregnancy was a mortal sin, and that any other position apart from the so-called 'natural' one (husband on top) was

at least a venial sin. St. Augustine taught that intercourse during pregnancy is gravely sinful, indeed a
greater sin than fornication, adultery or even incest,
provided that these are done with the intention of
producing a baby.

Cultural conditioning

These simple facts exemplify what has already been
explained in an earlier chapter about the cultural
conditioning of moral norms. The bible is not a code
of revealed morality with ready-made answers to
moral questions, so when it came to formulating
specific rules of practical morality, the people of God
in both old and new testaments and the church ever
since had to fall back on the wisdom of the time,
which, in the very nature of things also reflected the
ignorance and superstitions of the particular stage
of civilization. The negative elements of various
stages may have been dropped intellectually by later
generations, but in many instances their influence
continued in the form of basic attitudes that still color
people's understanding of sexuality.

Paul and the early Christians accepted the Stoic
philosophy of the time, which exalted nature, reason
and decorum, and downgraded the emotions and
feelings. This tradition was continued and intensi-
fied by Christian writers all through the history of
the church, until it reached a kind of rationalism in
the neo-scholastic period up to the Second Vatican
Council. A consequence of this was the almost morbid
distrust of venereal pleasure that is so marked a feature of most theological writing on sexuality. Another
element that entered in was the Manichean down-
grading of matter as evil. This came particularly
through the great Augustine and was compounded by
his own guilt-ridden experience of sexual intercourse

in an eleven-year, quasi-permanent union that had little of personal love in it. He held that there was nothing rational, spiritual or sacramental in the act of intercourse. It is easy to dismiss this view as a mere historical interlude, but there are some who still quote Augustine on marriage as though he were almost part of divine revelation. Vatican II has a very different view.

Anti-feminism

All through the centuries of tradition, reaching back into the old testament and beyond, there is a negative attitude to women and all things feminine. In spite of the Genesis account of the complementarity of the sexes, and the personal roles played by many women in the old testament, women were considered the property of men, with a utilitarian value. In its original context, the sixth commandment of the decalog was not concerned about sexual morality as much as with the injustice done to husband or father by the man who has unlawful relations with a girl. Jewish rabbis feared women as a distraction and temptation. In the Jewish tradition, women were generally considered greedy, curious, lazy, and jealous. Christian writers took over Aristotle's notion of the female as a half-baked man, a male *manqué*. Over a thousand years later, St. Thomas Aquinas found no reason to differ from this view or even question it; he accepted it as a fact of nature. With all the arrogance and simplicity of the male, he discussed whether women should have been created at all, and with colossal ignorance (natural enough for the time) he proclaimed that the female is something defective and *manqué*. He explained that the active power in the seed of the male tends to produce something like itself, perfect in masculinity; but the procreation of a female is the

result either of a weakness in the seed, of some un-
suitability of the material, or of some change brought
about by external influences such as the south wind.
Often quoted by church authorities as an oracle on
natural law, he maintained that even before original
sin, woman by nature would have been governed by
man for her own good, because the power of rational
discernment is by nature stronger in man.

Pessimistic bias

St. Paul could compare marriage to the union between
Christ and the church and vice versa. But no matter
how well the glories of Christian marriage were later
sung by the great doctors of the church, their pessi-
mism came through. According to Augustine, only
procreation could justify marriage, sex, or even wom-
en. Pope St. Gregory the Great affirmed that it was
as impossible to have intercourse without sin as it
was to fall into a fire and not burn. Clement of Alexandria compared marital intercourse to 'an incurable
disease, a minor epilepsy'. The great St. Jerome held
that virginity was the norm in paradise, that marriage
came about as a result of sin, and that the only good
in marriage is that it can give birth to virgins. In the
fifteenth century St. Bernardine of Siena claimed
that of 1000 marriages, 999 are of the devil's making.
One wonders how he did the survey. This was in the
'age of faith', when most of the known world was
Christian. The same saint, the greatest preacher in
Europe in his day, maintained that it was a piggish
irreverence and a mortal sin if husband and wife do
not abstain from intercourse for several days before
receiving holy communion. During the Middle Ages,
a woman who died in childbirth was often buried
in a special corner of the cemetery and without the
usual honors, though some theologians permitted

such a woman's burial in consecrated ground if the baby had first been cut out of the womb.

St. Augustine of Canterbury felt it necessary to write to Pope Gregory the Great to ask if it were permissible to baptize women when pregnant or during their monthly periods, and whether they could enter churches and receive communion at such times. The pope told him it was no sin, but in spite of this, Archbishop Theodore shortly afterwards forbade nuns and lay women to enter a church or take communion during their periods. The penalty for breaking the law was three days fasting on bread and water. The prohibition remained part of the general law of the church until the sixteenth century. This notion of ritual impurity infiltrated Christian thinking from pagan superstition, according to which terrible things were believed to happen when women touched anything during their periods: crops would dry up, fruit rot on the trees and iron would turn rusty. No one would claim that this kind of thinking is still at work in the church, but it is hard to avoid the impression that something of the basic negative attitude lurks behind even the idealistic language of modern church documents on the role of women, especially since it is taking us so long to give practical recognition to the equality of the sexes.

This negative attitude to women was reflected in the constitutions of many religious congregations of men. On the subject of chastity, monks were told that little need be said of this 'angelic' virtue, but they were advised to flee the company of women. If it was necessary or really useful to speak to them, conversation should be as brief as possible. They were told that since the Blessed Virgin was troubled and afraid at the approach of the angel, how much more they themselves, weak and shaking reeds, had reason to fear. However much they may have outgrown it, this was

the kind of writing that the majority of the world's
religious were brought up on.

Literal repetition

The more recent documents of the church show a radical advance on previous teaching insofar as they go
beyond the harsh dichotomy between sex primarily
for procreation and sex merely for pleasure. The fundamental importance of the sexual dimension of
human personality is explicitly recognized. But once
the realm of general principles is left behind, confusion returns. Not only official statements of church
authorities, but recently published textbooks of some
moral theologians, simply repeat the old black-and-
white prescriptions of sexual morality, with little
reference not only to the discoveries of the human
sciences, but even to developments in scripture studies, dogmatic and moral theology. It is taken for
granted that Augustine, Aquinas and other theologians were justified in laying down norms for Christian life on the basis of the contemporary outlook on
sexuality, seriously defective though it was, but
today's theologians seem to be denied this right and
duty.

Much of offical teaching simply repeats statements
from the past as though they could be valid for all
time, independently of historical and cultural developments and differences. It is frequently asserted
quite simply that the 'constant teaching of the church'
has condemned contraception, with no reference to
the fact that the problem could not possibly have
been understood in today's terms until the facts of
human reproduction had been discovered, within
the last century. The so-called 'safe period' was 'permitted' only with the greatest reluctance at first,
whereas now some preachers present it almost as one
of the glories of natural law, God's gift to women.

St. Jerome justified the prohibition of intercourse during menstruation for the good of the fetus. He argued that 'if a man copulates with a woman at that time, the fetuses conceived are said to carry the vice of the seed, so that lepers and giants are born from this conception, and the corrupted menses makes the foul bodies of either sex too small or too big.' This is a fair example of the guesswork that took the place of knowledge, but it was often on the basis of such defective knowledge of the facts of nature that moral norms were formulated. Perhaps the ignorance seldom went to the extreme of the Roman emperor who claimed that homosexuality was the cause of earthquakes, but there are enough bizarre examples in the history of the church to alert us to the need for critical reflection.

Physicalism

Following the method of Aristotle, the scholastic theologians of the Middle Ages used philosophical principles to reach truths that we know can be reached only through empirical observation. They maintained that the stars must be perfect spheres, whereas our telescopes reveal that they are not. They believed that the male seed was a human being in miniature and they knew nothing of the contribution of the female apart from her function as receptacle; our microscopes tell us a different story. Reverence for the 'little man' contained in the semen meant that any form of contraception was thought of in terms of murder rather than an exercise in responsible parenthood. That same reverence for the seed as bearer of life led to a continual concern about 'loss of seed' or 'waste of seed' which created endless scruples and dominated so much confessional practice in this area, whereas modern science shows that nature's own 'wastage' has truly astronomical proportions.

None of this outmoded 'science' is preserved in the church's more recent pronouncements, but the physicalism of their approach seems to indicate that they have not progressed far beyond it. Much of current teaching deals exclusively with the finality of the physical act of intercourse itself, in spite of the fact that the Vatican Council insisted that sexual morality is based on the nature of the person and his acts. The sexual act is discussed in isolation, with little or no reference to the psychological, personal and relational aspects, or to sexual maturity as a goal to be striven for over a period of time. It is said, for example, that both the magisterium of the church and the moral sense of the faithful have declared that masturbation is an intrinsically and seriously disordered act. The magisterium in this case is a letter of Pope Leo IX in 1054, a decree of the Holy Office in 1679, and speeches of Pope Pius XII in 1953 and 1956, none of which have an in-depth study of the problem or could take any account of today's insights into the nature and meaning of sexuality. Nowhere is it made clear how the 'moral sense of the faithful' is measured, since it is never consulted. This is not to say that masturbation is not a moral problem, but simply to point out that people are confused when it is decreed to be intrinsically and seriously disordered without any convincing explanation. Many would claim that the statement simply cannot be substantiated. The experience of vast numbers of the faithful is that the pastoral emphasis on this subject made their lives miserable for years on end and often made confession a torture.

If a text of the magisterium is to have such binding force, how are we to react to a decree of the Holy Office in 1666 (never revoked) which *condemned* a proposition saying that a kiss given for the pleasure of it is probably not a mortal sin but only a venial sin? Is it necessary to wait for another decree to tell us what most sensible Christians already know, namely that it is no sin at all, or at least that one cannot discuss the morality of it until the actual meaning of the particular kiss is known? There is no need to get upset about decrees like this, but they need to be seen in their cultural and theological context and interpreted accordingly. This does not mean that everything is relative, but only that we need to relativize some of our mistaken absolutes.

No consultation

A major weakness in the church's moral teaching, particularly in the area of sexuality, is that it is abstract and deductive, logically drawn from a theory of nature now seriously questioned and in many cases simply abandoned. It seems to take little account of what ought to be a central element in the discussion, namely how the faithful actually experience their sexuality. Celibate theologians should not _tell_ them what they experience or how they _should_ feel. Quite a number of people are now trusting their own experience and discovering that the news insights on the meaning of sexuality in terms of relationship and growth can give their Christian living a new depth. They are disturbed that theologians and church authorities can go on analyzing concepts and dogmatizing about sex without consulting Christian married people.

Barely two hundred years ago the influential theologian Billuart insisted that only procreative purpose could make intercourse lawful, that married people had to want children each time unless the act of intercourse was to be a sin. To the objection that the church allowed the old and sterile to marry, he replied that they could marry provided 'they intend to live chastely or use marriage by only returning but not demanding the debt'. Since these persons might commit

greater sins if they were not married, he taught that
it was better to 'dissimulate' the truth that they will
probably commit sin in marriage anyway. He went
on to say that 'even their confessors' must practice
this dissimulation. To the objection that his position
made marriage for anyone a continual occasion of sin,
which seemed 'hard, odious, and in some fashion
absurd', Billuart replied, 'I know this is true, not indeed precisely by reason of the state of matrimony,
but from the corruption of men.' Few modern theologians would be so arrogant or insensitive, but are
not some of today's moralists preaching from similar
ivory towers?

The ivory tower mentality of some moral theologians is not restricted to those who have been dead
for centuries. A random selection from manuals still
on the shelves of the clergy would frighten the laity.
A volume dealing with the sixth and ninth commandments has three pages on the virtue of chastity, one
of which is taken up with describing how virginity
is lost, and almost fifty pages listing in detail all the
possibilities of sexual sin, with their degrees of mortal
and venial. Without a blush of hesitation it says that
'company keeping with the intention of early marriage may be looked upon as a *necessary occasion of
sin*, and as far as sexual liberties are concerned,
engaged persons are *forbidden* to do anything which
is not permitted to other single people.' (Italics original). Is this how good Christian couples view their
relationship? Should they feel guilty if they fail to
share this attitude?

Signs of the times

It may seem that we have delayed too long with the
negative elements in our tradition, but it was necessary to bring them into the open and recognize them

publicly. The details have long been familiar to theologians and historians, but they are unknown to most of the faithful. Official statements from church authorities continue to express the most profoundly contradictory positions on sexuality, but the confusion in the documents is nothing compared to the confusion in the minds of people. The confusion would be unsettling enough if it were merely an intellectual muddle, but it is much more serious when it involves an agony of conscience compounded by emotional hang-ups and guilt-complexes. To realize how much of the traditional teaching in the area of sexuality is colored by influences that have nothing to do with the gospel, and so need to be re-evaluated today, is already a liberating experience. While learning from the valid insights and experience of history, we should never become imprisoned by the past. Neither the bible, church pronouncements or natural law provide a code of morality to be read to the faithful by experts who alone know how to read them. Jesus promised his followers that the Holy Spirit would lead them into all truth, so the whole church is a learning and pilgrim church. It is the whole Christian community together in dialog and prayer, men and women, who have to discover the meaning of sexuality today and formulate the principles that will guide them in its responsible use.

Sex is not the whole of life, but the sexual dimension of our human nature touches the deepest levels of our being, so it is understandable that it be a moral concern, not only for the teaching authorities in the church, but for Christians who want to love God and grow in his love as whole persons, as men and women. If they are to be helped, we need to explicitly disown the negative and pessimistic elements in our tradition, honestly admit the weakness of many of our positions in the past, and face up to the challenge

of making the Christian view of sexuality meaningful
in today's world. From what has been said in previous
chapters about the bible and the various types of law
in our understanding of morality, it should be clear
that a literal quotation of the past will not do. The
problems of human life cannot simply be brushed
aside by triumphantly brandishing a text from scripture or an ecclesiastical decree.

The Second Vatican Council speaks of reading the
signs of the times in the light of the gospel as a continuing sign of God's will. We are not doing this if we
dogmatize about sexual morality without any reference to our contemporary understanding and experience of sex. Quite radical developments have
taken place in the last few decades. The equality and
complementarity of the sexes, the personal dimensions of the sexual relationship, our growing control
over fertilization, the changing patterns of family
life, and the greater awareness of what marriage can
do in terms of deep personal fulfillment, are all factors
that must be taken into account before we can even
begin to talk about sexual morality.

Person-centered morality

To drop the negative and pessimistic 'do's and don'ts'
of the older approach is not to cut loose from all norms
and principles. It means to get away from the old
physicalism and the fragmented approach to human
actions, and to begin with the more basic question
of what sexuality is all about, what it means to be a
man or a woman, indeed what it means to be human.
The Second Vatican Council reminds us that sexual
morality is based on the nature of the human person,
so it can only be understood in human and personal
terms. It is true that man does have a certain nature
that sets limits upon him and defines his possibilities.
But it is not the nature of a ready-made being, already

fully defined, but of a being who must fashion his potentialities into a harmonious whole. Man must freely become what he is, so human sexuality involves freedom.

It is man himself who gives meaning and shape to his sexual drive. Norms of sexual behavior cannot, therefore, be established simply on the basis of biological laws, but will be shaped in accordance with man's growing understanding of himself and in the light of his experience. Once again, the historical dimension of morality enters in, because his self-understanding is growing, and his experience is changing. Vatican II quietly dropped the time-worn and misleading distinction between primary and secondary ends of marriage in its document on the *Church in the Modern World*, and produced a chapter on responsible parenthood and the relational aspect of sexuality that would have been condemned by the Holy Office less than forty years earlier. For Aquinas, 'primary' originally meant generic, what was common to both animal and human reproduction, while 'secondary' meant what was specific to humans, but the later tradition turned this upside down and took primary to mean more important, and secondary less important. It will take time before the new approach to the problems of sexuality is commonly accepted. The new approach will not be trapped into making long lists of laws covering every conceivable situation and describing the precise boundaries of the different degrees of sin. More searching questions will need to be asked about the *human meaning* of particular kinds of behavior, rather than simply the biological function of certain acts.

Sex as language

Morality is about becoming a person, and nobody grows alone. People need people. It is only through

relating to others that we grow in maturity and develop as persons. Our relationship is expressed and
grows through commmunication: by speech, gesture,
touch, working with and for others. Sexuality is part
of this language of communication, a very deep and
powerful part. Through it we can enter into varying
degrees of relationship with, and commitment to,
other people. The personalist approach to sexual
morality advocated by Vatican II means understanding sexuality as language, a form of communication.
Thus, the moral evaluation of any sexual expression
will depend on its truthfulness, whether or not it faithfully expresses the truth of the person and the particular relationship. Since relationship is a growing,
developing thing, from the casual acquaintance to the
total commitment of marriage, with its openness to,
and responsibility for, new life, there is a whole
sliding scale of what is appropriate or inappropriate,
truthful or deceitful, in the expressions of that relationship, both sexual and other.

The moral challenge in our use of sex is to keep it
meaningful, not to falsify or trivialize it. It is said to
be the easiest language to speak, but the most difficult
to make meaningful and to keep meaningful. The full
human meaning of intercourse is the whole person
saying with all his being, body, soul, mind and heart,
'I love you, you only, and you always'. Someone who
says this without being in a position to follow through
in commitment is saying more than he means. This im-
poverishes the sexual language to the point where
he can no longer say all that he means when he really
wants to and is in a position to. On a deeper level,
such a person will have so scattered his personal being
in isolated acts without meanings, that he will no
longer be capable of the total self-giving that is the
essence of sexual relations at their highest point of
intensity and fulfillment.

It might be feared that this new approach leads to individualism, that the individual can give any meaning he wishes to his actions. This can in fact happen. Sex can be for breeding, for fun, for revenge, for exploration or exploitation, for escape or for a variety of other purposes. But just as man is not free to create his own language (unless he wishes to talk only to himself) but learns the language of his community, so the community will already have established the essential meaning of sexual activity on the basis of its experience of human nature and its needs. It will have discovered that certain forms of sexual activity do not lead to growth in maturity and fulfillment, and so are considered cul-de-sacs, dead-ends. Others are part of the groping, experimental growing-up process, to be overcome and integrated into the mature personality. It will have discovered the emptiness and meaninglessness of sex isolated from its human context, the sadness of pornography, the banalization of sex that comes from a sex-obsessed culture.

Many of today's young people see sexual activity as an experience in closeness and intimacy, a protection and refuge against the loneliness of much of modern living. But deeper reflection will show that this is simply one more 'use' of sex. It can only banish the loneliness and isolation of the moment. It cannot of itself link past, present and future into the harmonious whole that is human life. The universal experience of mankind is that sex does not create friendship and intimacy, but that it needs the constancy, stability and commitment of real friendship in order to retain its power of true expression, to be the language of closeness, intimacy and love. Experience has also shown that the institution of marriage provides the best possibility for the protection and growth of such a relationship. This is not a popular truth in today's world of casual encounter, experimental sex, throwaway friends and disposable relationships, but it is one that the Christian community needs to proclaim from the housetops, not merely in words, but in the living sermon and quiet example of its married couples.

Wholeness and growth

It will be found that the 'new sexual ethic' already taking shape in the church, though not fully developed in official teaching, largely agrees with the traditional view on the essentials of sexual morality. It condemns pre-marital and extra-marital sex, and warns of the dangers of exploitation of persons in the use of sex, both within and outside of marriage. But it avoids the listing of physical actions as mortal or venial sins. While not ignoring the physical facts of nature and the biological laws, it assesses the morality of sexual behavior in the context of its appropriateness to persons in their wholeness and in their relationships.

The concepts of wholeness and growth are central to the new approach. The moral call is to grow into the fullness of the maturity of Christ by responding to those around us. Not all will be able to respond to the same degree, and we must beware of equating holiness with psychological wholeness. God's grace and love are available to all who open to him, though not all may be able to show it in their lives because of obstacles beyond their control. But within the limits of our ability we are expected to strive for whatever degree of wholeness is possible, and help others do the same by our response to them. This is what it means to love God 'with all our heart, with all our soul and with all our mind' and to love our neighbor as ourself. Wholeness refers to the totality of the human person, including the spiritual, intellectual, emotional and physical dimensions, in oneself and in others. To grow as a person is to develop all these harmoniously. To concentrate on any one of them (whether intellectual or sexual), at the expense of the others, is dehumanizing, depersonalizing, and this is sinful. It could even be said that some of the arguments of traditional moralists are seriously at fault here, since they allow biological processes to take precedence over personal and spiritual values.

The notion of growth is important because the individual is a developing being, and sexuality shares in this development. People move through various sexual stages, not only physically, but emotionally, psychologically, socially and spiritually. While all are called to use their sexuality in the service of responsible love, not all are capable of the same response at the same time, so a standard judgment for all is simply not possible.

It is beyond our purpose here to give a complete theology of sexuality, but it should be clear that if people are to be helped to integrate their sexuality into their growth as Christians, much of the older theology needs to be discarded. It is sad, though understandable, that so much of the church's energy in the past decade or so has been expended on the question of contraception, and sadder still that so much of the controversy centered more on authority than on the moral issue itself. Though it was agonizing for large numbers of married couples, it is not the most important question in Christian morality, nor even in sexual morality. The same may be said of pre-marital sex. We need to re-focus our moral vision so that we are not hypnotized by sex. We must realize that in spite of all the talk about the permissive society and the sexual revolution, for most people their sexual sins constitute only a very small proportion of their general burden of sinfulness.

No easy answers

We have already seen that if we could take the emphasis off law and precise measurement, people might have a more balanced and responsible approach to morality. This is particularly the case in the area of sexuality. There would be less confusion, fear and scruple about sin. Some would need to learn to live with a degree of uncertainty, but the experience of some spiritual tension would bring a touch of realism and seriousness to their moral striving. It would be a disservice to them to introduce a new legalism by listing specific acts as mortal and venial sins, and outlining what is now 'permitted' in the various zones of the body. Instead, we have the far more difficult task of explaining the Christian meaning of sex, providing them with the know-how of the decision-making process, and trusting them to use their conscience as they make their personal choices. We can invite them to reflect, and give them pointers for their reflection.

There may still be simple people who prefer just to be 'told' what is right and wrong, but it is an abdication of authority and spiritual leadership to look on them as the ideal and to wish that all were like them. The church is a community in which people should grow and be helped to grow. Part of that helping is to provide them with the facts about the meaning of scripture, the nature and extent of the church's teaching authority, the purpose and limitations of law, the historical development of moral norms, and the discoveries of the human sciences. Knowledge like this may free them from pseudo-sins (like sexual thoughts being automatically bad thoughts), and alert them to the more serious questions they should be asking themselves, questions to which there may be no easy, black-and-white answers.

6

MY CONSCIENCE OR THE LAW?

There are large numbers of Catholics to whom it comes as a profound and disturbing shock to be told that there are moral questions for which there are no black-and-white answers. Believing in the one true church, with its divinely-revealed deposit of faith, they were given the impression that there was a Catholic position on everything from bus-driving to bee-keeping, and a Catholic solution to every moral and social problem. Of course, they believed in conscience, and were aware that they had an obligation to follow it. But the obligation applied only to an *informed* conscience, and the information would be supplied by the church, which provided the objective moral norms. The function of conscience was to know the moral principles, the rules of right and wrong, judge which ones applied to the particular case, and then decide how they were to be obeyed according to the circumstances of the situation.

For many such people, the controversies of the past decade were confusing and upsetting, particularly the contraception debate. They suddenly discovered that the information they were given was no longer as clear as they would like, and that it was being variously interpreted, not only by laity but by priests, bishops and indeed whole hierarchies. Quoting Vatican II, many priests told them they should 'follow their conscience'. But this was not particularly helpful since they had always believed that following one's conscience meant accepting the teaching of the church, and to do otherwise would be simply disobedience, a sin, using the excuse of conscience to do your own thing, to please yourself. This attitude is not restricted to the

simple faithful, but seems to be shared by a considerable number of priests and bishops. It is generally
accepted that Vatican II admitted the principle of
freedom of conscience, indeed proclaimed it as a basic
human right. But there is still a huge gap between
the national assent people give to this on the surface
of their minds, and the real assent it calls for in personal conviction and practical acceptance of all its
consequences. It is sad, though understandable, that
years after the Council it should still be necessary to
spell out the role of conscience in the moral life.

Loyalty or confrontation

That there could be any conflict between conscience
and authority in the church seemed unthinkable until
fairly recently, apart from extreme cases, and even
there authority was always presumed to have been in
the right. One recalls the exhortations to loyalty by
preachers in the period immediately before *Humanae
Vitae*, telling people to accept the decision of the Holy
Father whenever it came, *whatever it might be*. Such
preaching was well-intentioned, concerned with the
common good of the church, but reflected a theology of
conscience, authority and indeed morality that falls
far short of Vatican II principles. It was taken for
granted that right and wrong can simply be *decreed*
and must be blindly accepted. During that same period
busy pastors and confessors were heard to complain
impatiently about the contraception debate: 'why
can't those people in Rome tell us what's right and stop
all the nonsense'.

Another aspect of the tension between conscience and
authority, and of the inadequate theology of conscience so
common in the church, became obvious in the years
immediately following *Humanae Vitae*. Confrontation
between individual bishops and their priests, and

between priests and laity, ended in head-on collisions in which people were deeply wounded and some were scarred for life. For the traditionally-minded, these sad episodes were simply cases of normal authority dealing with disobedience. But developmental psychologists tell us that the earliest and most elementary response to authority tends to be blind and automatic, and since we all carry within us the child we once were, in situations of stress we revert to childish levels. Both civil and religious leaders tend to rely on this primitive form of response and insist on it when under attack, rather than exercise true leadership by promoting autonomous moral decision. Perhaps this is an over-simplified and one-sided reading of these sad incidents, but people are confused when they are given the impression that on moral grounds they can say No to a civil regime, but a situation can never arise where they may have to say a personal, conscientious No to an ecclesiastical authority. That there can be dissent, and indeed loyal dissent, not only *in*, but *for* the church, is not easily understood.

Confusion about conscience

That Vatican II's notion of conscience should be one of the least appreciated of the Council's insights is understandable. The very objectively-orientated theology that dominated the church's thinking for centuries made it difficult for people to think of conscience except in terms of obedience. If 'reality' was simply 'out there' to be accepted, studied, and contemplated, the laws of reality and morality were likewise already there, only to be read off and obeyed. Man the subject, the person, tended to be seen as an object among the other objects of creation, rather than as a self-determining person sharing in God's own creativity. The emphasis on law and measurement that was so large a feature of the church's practice gave the impression of absolute clarity and certainty, so that difficulties could only arise from subjective elements. The ideal was to overcome these and bring one's thought and action into line with 'the church'. This is not a criticism of the church's teaching or practice, but simply a statement of fact, of how things were.

However, a more general reason why there is so much confusion about the meaning of conscience, and difficulty in accepting Vatican II's principles, is that the vast majority of people, irrespective of whether they are Christians or not, have not progressed beyond Kohlberg's 'fourth stage' of moral development. Some spend their whole lives doing what they are told by authority simply out of fear. This is stage one, where we all begin as children, fearing punishment. Others obey because it brings them pleasure; this is stage two. Others are at stage three, where they obey because the group expects it, and they enjoy the esteem of their peers and are loyal to them. Stage four is that of most people, who obey simply because it is the law. They obey even when there is no pleasure in it and even when others ridicule them and disobey. The law is seen as good, because it is society's law, for the common good. At this stage, the ideal conscience is that of the law-abiding person. But some move beyond this stage to see the values the law is intended to promote and protect, and realize that mature conscience is not simply a matter of internalizing the law itself, but of being committed to a personal belief in the value behind it.

Levels of conscience

Of course, the word 'conscience' can be used in different senses, but all of them involve two basic elements: knowledge and obligation. We *know* that certain actions are right or wrong and we feel an *obligation* to act in accordance with this knowledge. When we do what we believe to be the right thing, we experience peace and satisfaction. When we go against our 'better judgment' we feel guilt and remorse. In ordinary experience, conscience is felt as a judgment in a concrete situation. I can continue working on this chapter or I can go and watch TV, but I know that I should continue working if I am to keep my promise to send it to the editor by the end of the week. Not only do I *know* that to continue is the right thing to do just now, but I also know that I *ought* to do so, no matter how much my tiredness or laziness tempt me away. In this sense, and on this level, conscience is always concerned with the concrete decision about what is to be done here and now.

But there is a deeper level presupposed by this particular judgment. Even before I arrive at the decision that to continue working is the right thing for me to do just now, I know that as a general principle it is a good thing to keep promises, that promises *ought* to be kept. Society depends to a large extent on people being faithful to their commitments, keeping their word. This level of conscience is our general knowledge of moral principles of right and wrong, good and bad. Depending on the individual, it can be more or less extensive. It includes the basic principles: do good rather than evil, treat others as you would wish to be treated yourself, and can extend to the ten commandments and specific developments of them. But it is more than neutral, speculative knowledge. It calls to something deep within our nature, stirs us with the conviction that we must obey it if we are to be true to ourselves. In this sense, conscience extends to a much deeper level than intellect and will, knowledge and consent. On this deepest of all levels, conscience is the core of our being as free persons. Here it can be said that 'conscience is the man'. It is on this level that the 'basic option' or 'fundamental attitude' spoken of in chapter 4 finds its context.

Man is not a finished article, possessing a ready-made nature, but a being of possibilities with a built-in call to grow in wholeness, to become actually what he is potentially. This forward and upward thrust is part of our God-given nature. The possibilities for good that we see before us summon us as the voice of conscience. Part of us reaches out ahead of the rest as we discern the good we ought to do, so we experience a certain stretching and tension, the tension of being challenged to grow. Good choices and right decisions in concrete situations enable the rest of our being to catch up, so to speak, with the part that reaches forward, so the tension is relieved, we are 'at one' with ourselves, and we experience not only growth, but peace and wholeness. This is the experience of a 'good conscience'.

When we ignore or refuse to do what we know we should, the tension remains, so we lose our basic oneness, we are torn within ourselves, we experience alienation and guilt. This is sin. It is a basic inconsistency between our knowing and our doing, and so we become divided within. We may make excuses for ourselves, rationalize our failure, but the very attempt to 'rationalize', to give 'reasons' for something which is really against reason, only makes more explicit our alienation and loss of oneness. Since we are not self-sufficient atoms, but relational beings, the sin and lack of oneness within ourselves spills over into our relationships. Whatever the occasion or the area of our sin, it cannot be confined or contained. Not only are we not at peace within ourselves, but on a deep level we become alienated from our fellowmen and from God. Even the material world that God meant to be our home and garden becomes a hostile environment to aggravate our inner lack of harmony. This is the 'bad conscience' that follows sin.

Self-awareness

On the deepest level of our personality, then, conscience is a special kind of self-awareness. It is a consciousness, not only of what we are doing, but of what we are and of what we are becoming. It tells us the kind of person we are, but at the same time it also tells us the kind of person we ought to be. It discloses the gap between the two. In this sense, it is not only a mirror or indicator, but also an invitation and a summons, commanding us *to become* and *to be* what we are meant to be. Since God is the author of our nature, it is God himself who calls us through the basic thrust of that nature, through the irrepressible appetites of mind, heart and body, recognized in the experience of conscience.

It is to this level of conscience that Jeremiah referred when he spoke in God's name: 'I will put my law within them, and write it on their hearts' (31:33), and the same message came through Ezekiel: 'I will give them a new heart and a new mind' (11:39). That God's call is not restricted to a particular religious group, but is addressed to all men in their very nature through the voice of conscience, is made clear by Paul, when he says that the conduct of the gentiles shows that 'what the law commands is written in their hearts. Their consciences also show that this is true, since their thoughts sometimes accuse them and sometimes defend them' (Rom 2:15). Since the gentiles knew nothing of the Jewish law, Paul is referring to something much deeper, to the experience of conscience itself.

This insight of Paul is echoed by the Second Vatican Council, speaking of the salvation of non-Christians in its *Dogmatic Constitution on the Church:* 'Those who, through no fault of their own, do not know the gospel of Christ or his church, but who nevertheless seek God with a sincere heart, and, moved by grace, try in their actions to do his will as they know it through the dictates of their conscience - they too may achieve eternal salvation' (n.16).

Vatican II

The Council uses the word 'conscience' no less than seventy two times in eleven of its seventeen documents. Thirty eight of these occur in the pastoral constitution on *The Church in the Modern World*, and thirteen in the declaration on *Religious Freedom*.

This is not the place to analyze all these passages, but the essentials may be seen in one or two quotations. The first chapter of *The Church in the Modern World* gives a beautiful picture of man created in the image of God, though spoiled by sin, and speaks of the essential unity of man's nature, of the dignity of the intellect, of truth, and of wisdom, of the dignity of the moral conscience, and of the excellence of freedom. This is the context in which the Council presents its understanding of conscience. 'Deep within his conscience man discovers a law which he has not laid upon himself, but which he must obey. Its voice, ever calling him to love and to do what is good and to avoid evil, tells him inwardly at the right moment: do this, shun that. For man has in his heart a law inscribed by God. His dignity lies in observing this law, and by it he will be judged. His conscience is man's most secret core, and his sanctuary. There he is alone with God, whose voice echoes in his depths' (n.16).

This text echoes many of the points we have already made. It makes clear that conscience is knowledge, awareness of a special kind, namely the consciousness of being obliged by a law not of our own making, yet within ourselves. That law is the innate thrust of our nature to love the good and avoid evil. This directive of our nature is permanent, ongoing, but not specified in detail as to what precisely is good or evil. But from time to time, 'at the right moment', the obligation becomes specific to do this or avoid that. The text says nothing about how we discover and decide in the concrete what is right or wrong. That the law 'written in man's heart' is simply a metaphor should be clear from chapter 3 above. What this metaphor refers to is man's unrestricted desire to know and the urge to make one's activity consistent with one's knowing. This urge is the inclination towards wholeness, 'at-oneness' with oneself, peace and harmony within oneself.

Conscience a sanctuary

The 'law in man's heart' is written there by God insofar as God is the author of man's nature. Man's dignity lies in observing this law, that is to say that man is only true to himself when he acts in accordance with what his conscience tells him is right. That he will be judged on the basis of his fidelity to conscience is a reminder that morality is part of religion. The text says quite clearly that he will be judged, not according to rules he learned by heart, or the views of his parents, or ecclesiastical documents, or laws from the bible, or even some law in God's mind if it could be read, but according to his own personal conscience, not according to whether he did the right thing, but basically according to whether he did *what he saw and understood* as the right thing. Man's actions are judged for the light they throw on his mind and heart, insofar as they show the kind of person he is. But it is really man himself who is judged. His conscience is thus said to be his secret core, his innermost being. It is an area so intimate that only God can penetrate it, God who alone can read man's heart. It is man's sanctuary, a sacred place not to be violated, a place where man can take refuge from all but himself and God.

For all men

The voice of God that is heard there is not a detailed code, a dictated law, but rather the consciousness that morality is not simply convenience, efficiency or utility, but a demand of God himself as to what he wants us to be. For the Christian, this is *explicit* in his belief that in Jesus, God our Father calls us to be his children, and expects us to live 'with that mind which was in Christ Jesus'. It is *explicit* insofar as what we see to be the right thing to do is understood explicitly as what God wants us to do. For the non-believer, God's voice is *implicit* insofar as his moral consciousness is tinged with religious consciousness as he discovers the absoluteness of the moral call through conscience, and finds himself grasped by an ultimate concern.

The Council makes clear that conscience is not the exclusive prerogative of Christians, and that Christians have no monopoly of wisdom when it comes to knowing right and wrong, though our faith can provide us with a new context and motivation for our moral striving. The text continues: 'Through loyalty to conscience, Christians are joined to other men in the search for truth and for the right solution to many moral problems which arise both in the life of individuals and from social relationships.' (n.16). The voice of conscience, therefore, does not answer our questions or solve our problems in advance. There still remains the demanding task of discovering the right thing to do. Though utterly personal, conscience is not meant to function in isolation from others. The search for what is right is a continuing process in which we share with others, with all men of good will. That it is a process rather than a static possession is clear from the following sentence: 'The more a correct conscience prevails, the more do persons and groups turn aside from blind choice and try to be guided by the objective standards of moral conduct.' (n. 16). Correct conscience is not instantly established by being told the right thing to do. Rather it is gradually attained insofar as people move away from blind choice and are guided by objective standards, and on the other hand, to the extent that people try to be guided by objective standards, their choices will not be blind, but governed by reason.

Objective norms

The reference to 'objective standards of moral conduct' or 'objective moral norms' could give the impression that correct conscience means simply acceptance of, and obedience to, a law laid down by some authority. This is not the case. It means rather that the reasons for claiming that a particular action is the right one must be good reasons, not mere whim, that in one's search for the right thing to do, one will be faithful to the laws of reason, be conscious of the dangers of prejudice, bias, selfishness, be aware of one's obligations and commitments, of the possible consequences of one's action, of the effect it will have on other people, etc. These are all *objective norms*, in the light of which one discovers the right thing to do in a concrete situation. The guidelines provided by laws are an important factor in our deliberation, and in most cases we need little discussion to realize that obedience to the law is the responsible and right thing to do. But there are vast areas of life not covered by any law apart from the most general principles that we should not exploit others, that we should treat them as we would wish to be treated ourselves. In those areas where there is a specific law, there may be occasions when conscience will dictate that we disobey it in the name of a higher law, in the name of justice and in the name of God. It would be a misuse of this text of the Council to claim that a person in this situation is simply deciding for himself apart from the 'objective moral norm'.

The text speaks of right conscience knowing the objective norms, but it is clear that knowledge is not virtue. It is not enough simply to know what principles apply, one must 'try to be guided' by them, the implication being that this is not always easy. Effort is needed to put them into practice in trying to discover what is right, and further effort is required to decide to *do* what conscience dictates. Doing what conscience dictates as the right thing to do is virtuous action. Acting against conscience is moral wrongdoing, moral evil, or in religious terms 'sin'.

Mistaken conscience

The Council acknowledges that one may be mistaken as to what is really the right thing to be done, that what one decides in all good faith may in reality turn out to be a bad thing. But even in this case, one is still obliged to be consistent with oneself, to act in accordance with one's honest conviction. Even in error, the sanctity of conscience remains intact. But there is an obligation to do one's best to keep conscience alive and healthy, delicately sensitive to objective norms and to the true good of the human person. The paragraph concludes: 'Yet it often happens that conscience goes astray through ignorance which it is unable to avoid, without thereby losing its dignity. This cannot be said of the man who takes little trouble to find out what is true and good, or when conscience is by degrees almost blinded through the habit of committing sin.' (n.16).

The sanctity of conscience is further emphasized in the following paragraph, under the heading: the excellence of freedom. 'It is, however, only in freedom that man can turn himself towards what is good . . . That which is truly freedom is an exceptional sign of the image of God in man. For God willed that man should 'be left in the hand of his own counsel' so that he might of his own accord seek his creator and freely attain his full and blessed perfection by cleaving to him. Man's dignity therefore requires him to act out of conscious and free choice, as moved and drawn in a personal way from within, and not by blind impulses in himself or by mere external constraint. Man gains such dignity when, ridding himself of all slavery to the passions, he presses forward towards his goal by freely choosing what is good, and, by his diligence and skill, effectively secures for himself the means suited to this end.' (n.17) That freedom is essential to the exercise of conscience is stressed in the declaration on *Religious Freedom*: Man 'is bound to follow his conscience faithfully in all his activity so that he may come to God, who is his last end. Therefore he must not be forced to act contrary to his conscience. Nor must he be prevented from acting according to his conscience, especially in religious matters.' (n.3)

This applies even to the erroneous conscience. Quoting the example of the apostles and the early church, who steadfastly preached the gospel but did not impose it by coercion, the Council says that 'at the same time, however, they showed respect for the weak even though they were in error, and in this way made it clear how 'each of us shall give account of himself to God' (Rom 14:12) and for that reason is bound to obey his conscience.' (n.11)

Sanctity of conscience

This emphasis on the sanctity and freedom of conscience was heady stuff for a number of people, who, with only a superficial acquaintance with the Council documents, began invoking conscience almost daily to justify their eccentricities. The Council itself was well aware of this danger, and indeed adverted to it explicitly in the declaration on *Religious Freedom*. But notwithstanding the possibility of misunderstanding and abuse, it did not water down its basic teaching on the dignity, rights and obligations of conscience. It is clear from its text that the morally mature person is not the 'yes-man' beloved by some authorities, but the one who can form his own judgments in the light of truth and objective reality. 'Modern man is subjected to a variety of pressures and runs the risk of being prevented from following his own free judgment. On the other hand, there are many who, under the pretext of freedom, seem inclined to reject all submission to authority and make light of the duty of obedience. For this reason this Vatican Council urges everyone, especially those responsible for educating others, to try to form men with a respect for the moral order who will obey lawful authority and be lovers of true freedom - men, that is, who will form their own judgment in the light of truth, direct their activities with a sense of responsibility, and strive for what is true and just in willing cooperation with others.' (n.8)

A basic right

These statements are not true simply because the Vatican Council decreed them to be so. The Council itself acknowledges that freedom of conscience and of honest conviction is one of the basic rights of man, that it is rooted in the very dignity of the person, 'the demands of which have become more fully known to human reason through centuries of experience' (Religious Freedom, n.9) It is a right to be respected by all men, but 'Christians are bound to respect it all the more conscientiously' (ibid).

The Council caught most people unprepared for the new insights, and in the confusion of the post-conciliar period it is understandable that many should come to think of conscience and authority as being necessarily opposed. In fact, they are complementary aspects of the same basic search for the human good. Whether in the church or in civil society, authority is simply the voice of the community deciding what is right, what is the best thing for all concerned. The morally mature and responsible person will admit that there is a presumption in favor of authority and law, that even though it may not be the absolute best, it is still good, and normally should be obeyed. The body of laws constitute a kind of traditional wisdom or conventional morality that grew out of the conscience and experience of the community. But it can also happen that they reflect the narrow-mindedness and prejudice of a particular community, as in the case of racialist and discriminatory laws. Unless individuals could challenge the commonly accepted moral standards of their society and refuse to be mere conformists, there would never be any moral progress; man would still be in the jungle. If society today is more sensitive to and concerned about the dignity of the human person and the equality of all men, it is only because there were prophetic voices down through history to protest against exploitation and discrimination, and to rebel against even lawful authority.

It would be a mistake to imagine that this holds true only with regard to civil laws, that conscience could not clash with ecclesiastical authority. History proves the contrary. The laws of the church are not divinely-revealed absolutes, but human ordinances for the supernatural good of the community of believers. As such, they reflect not only the wisdom of the church at a given time, but also the cultural and theological outlook of a particular period, with all its limitations. It is instructive to read a list of the propositions that the faithful were expected to hold down through the centuries. A few of the more bizarre ones have been quoted in an earlier chapter. Even those decreed within the present century make one wonder. Most of them were never officially withdrawn, so in theory they are still the 'official position' of the church. It was decreed that the gospels were written in the same sequence in which we enumerate them today, that the Pentateuch was written entirely by Moses, that most of the psalms were composed by David, that the epistle to the Hebrews was written by Paul. Not one of these statements is taken seriously today. One would have been called a modernist, and therefore condemned, for suggesting that the Holy Office might be changed or that the Index of Forbidden Books be abolished. Yet, the Index has in fact gone, and the Holy Office has been changed.

A service to the church

Does it follow that one is not free to dissent from any of these positions until they are withdrawn? Such an attitude would do violence to reason itself. Respect for authority demands that its laws be accepted with reverence, that its teaching be received with docility, but one is still bound by the dictates of conscience guided by objective norms. No church authority can order a member of the faithful to close his mind, so anyone convinced of the falsity of this or that doctrinal decree has the right to hold his conviction and to explain the reasons for his stand. Had nobody ever done this, the church would have suffered serious loss in the course of its history.

There is no shortage of examples to choose from, even apart from the Galileo fiasco. To speak of collegiality in the church was tantamount to heresy up to less than thirty years ago. Had everybody accepted this position without question, it would not have been possible for the Vatican Council to produce the dogmatic constitution on *The Church* as it did. Had nobody ever broken liturgical laws in the forties and fifties, it is unlikely that the liturgical renewal launched by the Council would have taken place. It was the constant teaching of the church for over fourteen hundred years that slavery was not intrinsically evil. This was not officially changed until Vatican II, but it would never have changed had not conscientious people spoken out against it. An acquaintance with history and a more nuanced understanding of the teaching authority of the church might have cooled the contraception debate considerably.

Theological censorship was exercised in such a way in the church for the past four hundred years that there was a real lack of freedom of theological expression. Books were placed on the Index *en bloc*, with no discussion of their contents. Because of the severity of the censorship, moral theology as expounded in textbooks for generations was largely thoughtless conformism. That the climate in today's church is different is due to the fact that there were conscientious non-conformists to ask questions and look for reasons. To be faithful to conscience, therefore, is not simply to go one's own way in spite of the church, but to be faithful to the reality of the church, which is Christ, to contribute to the welfare of the church, and to build up the faith of the community. It is not merely the exercise of a personal right, but a vital contribution to the life of the church.

Conscience not infallible

But Vatican II's insistence on the sacredness of the individual conscience should not allow us to forget that conscience is not infallible, that it can be blunted by sin, and that even good men can be guilty of self-deception. There is wisdom in the old saying that no one is a judge in his own case. But the solution is not that he should therefore abdicate his moral responsibility and let someone else take the place of his conscience. Rather, when he finds himself perplexed or in conflict with authority, he should look to his fellowmen for counsel, seek guidance from the bible and church teaching, and turn to God in prayer. All of these may enlighten him as to his own ignorance or self-deception, and he must always remain open to this possibility. But should he find that, having done everything possible, he is still convinced that he cannot accept the ruling of authority, this is the conviction he is bound to follow. Should this mean losing his reputation, his standing in the community, or even his life, his conscience is still the voice he must obey. No church, no authority, no superior can take its place.

Because the individual conscience is so open to distortion and self-deception and therefore may often be in error, and because there is normally a presumption in favor of authority, it is sometimes taken for granted that authority is automatically right, that dissent is simply disloyalty and disobedience, therefore sinful. But there is no principle in the bible or church teaching to the effect that authority is always right, or that the conservative side must always win. In fact, the language of winning or losing is totally out of place here, especially in the Christian community of the church. Since both authority and conscience are complementary elements in community living, it is not surprising that people should experience a tension between them. But this tension is something we must learn to live with. It can become almost unbearable for either side at times, and there is a natural inclination to get rid of it by bulldozer tactics. Authority may rigidly insist on conformity, or the individual may reject all dialog and make his decisions in isolation.

Situations like this can involve sin, on the part of either or both sides. If the non-conforming individual is sometimes intemperate or violent in his relations with authority, it may simply be the reaction of his sinful human nature to the violence originally done to his conscience and his human dignity. Violence breeds violence, and there are more kinds than physical assault. No one has a monopoly of sin any more than any one side has a monopoly of grace or inspiration. The church which is not only an institution with its necessary organization, but also a fellowship of brothers and sisters in the Lord, needs to discover ways and means of resolving conflicts, and exercise the ministry of reconciliation rather than the strategy of unconditional surrender.

7

AM I REALLY GUILTY?

Conscience, sin, guilt - these three terms are inevitably linked in any discussion of morality. The simple catechism presentation of them made their meaning quite clear. *Conscience* judges when an action is right or wrong, in accordance with God's law or not. To act against this judgment knowingly and deliberately, is sin. The awareness of having sinned is the voice of conscience telling us we are guilty, and this spills over into the emotions to create the *feeling* of *guilt*, though of course guilt itself is simply the other side of moral consciousness. This, in fact, is the experience of the normal person trying to live a good life. But for many people today, the terms are no longer as clear and simple as they used to be.

Brainwashing?

There are those who claim that there would be no experience of sin and guilt were it not for the indoctrination and brainwashing of children by the conventions and taboos of society. It is said that conscience is no more than Freud's *super-ego*, with its litany of do's and don'ts to tyrannize over us and make us feel guilty. It is simply the finger-wagging parent, no longer supervising potty training, but now internalized to hound us even in our secret thoughts and hidden desires. The all-seeing eye of an avenging God is simply the religious extension of this.

Psychiatrists can tell of the high percentage of their patients who are crippled by a burden of neurotic guilt that has little to do with real sin and moral conscience. On the other hand, so much is now known of the limitations of human freedom that come from our physical make-up, psychological blocks, subtle social pressures and even the material environment in which we live, that people ask if we are really free in any meaningful sense of the word. If we are not free, we cannot be held responsible, so there is little room for sin or guilt. If sin is to be made meaningful in today's world, some of the confusion must be removed from the related areas of conscience, guilt, freedom and responsibility.

Real guilt and feelings

The world 'guilt' is used in a variety of senses. In general, it means the state of having committed a specified or implied offense. A distinction is sometimes made between *subjective* and *objective* guilt, depending on whether the person concerned subjectively feels guilty, or it is imputed to him by others. If a law has been broken, we speak of *legal* guilt, admitted or proved. When the wrongdoing is considered a moral evil or sin, we speak of *moral* guilt. But in the strict sense moral guilt can never be merely objective, or imputed by others, since the moral meaning and evaluation of a particular action necessarily involves the person's intention and freedom. Society can say that murder, adultery, lying, etc. are wrong, and condemn them as such, but it cannot point to an individual and say that he is in sin. Only God, or the individual himself, can make this judgment. *Subjective* guilt, on the other hand, is the personal awareness of having done wrong, or the belief (possibly mistaken) that one has done wrong. This awareness is not simply a cold, clinical knowledge, but usually involves *feelings* of uneasiness and remorse. Subjective guilt may be normal, rational, based on the knowledge of real wrongdoing for which one was responsible, or that morbid, neurotic state of emotional disturbance unrelated to any wrongdoing, or out of all proportion to the wrong done.

Another way of looking at the distinction between subjective and objective is to consider the *inner* element and the *social* element in guilt. The social element is to be found in legal or juridical guilt, and involves making compensation or being subject to a penalty for the wrong done. If the moral guilt has been repented and forgiven, for example in confession, the legal guilt remains until compensation or fine has been paid. The inner element is the psychological state of the person experiencing guilt, and this may be real moral guilt, as explained above, or simply neurotic feelings of guilt.

The distinction between healthy and morbid, normal and abnormal, is clear enough in principle, but can be confusing in practice. One of the reasons for this may be that not many people reach a high degree of moral maturity, and even when they do, they still carry within themselves the infant and adolescent they once were, and can be troubled by ghosts from the past. Guilt feelings thus become a prominent feature of the moral life. Another reason may be a certain imbalance in the church's teaching and preaching, relying too much on fear and threat of punishment. This causes anxiety, which is fertile soil for guilt feelings. The emphasis on law and the concern with precise measurement aggravates the tendency to scrupulosity, which is also a great source of exaggerated guilt feelings. Furthermore, the sexual dimension of life is already a difficult area to navigate in, but when it becomes the central concern of morality, as it is for many people, and as it is often preached, it adds its own turbulent and mysterious force to the experience of guilt. All of these can reinforce the notion of a taskmaster God easily vexed and quick to punish, and so we get a spiralling vicious circle of fear and guilt.

Super-ego and conscience

It would be wrong to assume, however, that the morally mature person is above all this, that conscience is simply a matter of intellectual judgment above and apart from the rest of the person. This latter notion is more akin to Freud's *super-ego*. The discoverer of psycho-analysis arrived at the concept of the super-ego by noticing that psychotic patients often had the delusion of being watched. They believed that people were waiting for them to do something forbidden so that they could be punished. From this, Freud formed the idea of a self above the normal self, a *super-ego* judging the self as an object. In early life this super-ego is formed by internalizing the attitudes and rules of parents, and as time goes on the young person accepts these personally, along with the conventions of society, and gradually the super-ego takes on all the functions of early authority figures: observing, accusing, punishing or rewarding.

There is enough truth in this for some psychiatrists to identify super-ego and conscience. Indeed the childish, immature conscience of many people has all the characteristics of Freud's super-ego, but the notion of conscience outlined in the previous chapter is different. The super-ego contains unconscious as well as conscious elements, but though mature conscience may feel the influence of unconscious factors, it is not determined by them. It makes its judgment in the light of consciously recognized and rationally evaluated circumstances. When it judges that wrong has been done, sin committed, the person *feels* guilt and remorse, realizes that it needn't have been so, and accepts responsibility for the sin. He experiences

inner alienation, lack of one-ness and general dishar-
mony within himself. But he does not punish himself
inordinately or torment himself with irrational fears.
He knows he can repent, be forgiven, repair the dam-
age, recover his peace of mind, and continue to grow.
As a Christian he knows that he is still loved by God,
that he doesn't have to *earn* that love, but simply
respond to it, and that the appropriate response in
sin is repentance and the acceptance of God's gift of
forgiveness.

Normal and abnormal

The super-ego is quite normal and natural in the
child. Indeed, it is the basis on which conscience will
later develop. The mature conscience outgrows it, but
many people never fully leave it behind. It begins with
the child's first experience of itself and its relation
to its parents. This first experience is of the human
being's most basic need, the need to be loved, be accepted, get approval. Side by side with this, there is
the fear of rejection. This can cause such terror that
it is felt as a threat to life itself. So powerful is this
fear that it conditions the child's learning process. The
child quickly learns what behavior brings approval,
acceptance and love, and what actions earn disap-
proval and cause feelings of rejection. This 'learning'
extends all the way from toilet training to table manners and the moral principles of right and wrong. The
latter are accepted without being fully understood,
simply in order to retain the approval and love of the
parents. When the child disobeys, it experiences guilt
feelings, not because of any appreciation of the wrong-
ness of the action, but because of the fear of rejection.
    The conditioning is so successful that the child
gradually internalizes the rules laid down by parents,
so that even when the parents are no longer present,

disobedience brings on the feeling of not being loved or lovable, a feeling of badness. This feeling is hard to bear, so the individual resorts to a variety of ways to earn approval, to win back the lost love or at least escape from the bad feeling. He can confess and look for reconciliation, or simply punish himself internally with guilt feelings. The guilt is often compounded by feelings of anger, at himself for his failure, at others in general, or at authorities for burdening him with the super-ego. Another escape from the pain of guilt is to project onto others the fault or evil discovered in oneself. Hatred of self quickly leads to hatred of others.

Psychiatrists are familiar with even more extreme forms and manifestations of guilt feelings. But from all of this it does not follow that conscience is simply a matter of conditioning. Neurotic guilt feelings can be traced to a variety of factors. They are more likely to be found in certain types of people, among introverts more than extroverts, and especially in people who experienced an insecure childhood, who lacked a sense of basic trust, whose parents were themselves insecure, rigid, overbearing, or perfectionist. Such people are predisposed to inordinate and often neurotic guilt feelings, and the guilt is further compounded when their experience of religion is one of rigid conformity to rules, and God is pictured in terms of threat and punishment. It can be said that such suffering is the result of conditioning. But not all conditioning is bad.

Healthy conditioning

Education involves a certain amount of conditioning, and the formation of conscience is no exception. The young child learns patterns of behavior on the basis of reward and punishment. 'Good' behavior brings approval and love, 'bad' behavior brings feelings of badness, guilt, rejection. Children conform on the basis of fear or pleasure. This is the pre-moral level of conscience. But gradually the young person moves beyond this to the stage of conventional role-conformity, where he tries to please others and be accepted by them. Here he is considering others, but his motive is still self-centered, in order to win their approval.

A further stage is reached when he acts out of respect for authority. At this stage moral obligation is equated with duty to social and religious authorities. Psychologists claim that most people operate at this level of conscience, which explains their preoccupation with law and obedience. A higher level is reached by those who act on the basis of self-accepted moral principles, who can be obedient to law and respect authority, but who are more concerned with the values behind the law.

This sequence of stages in the development of conscience is now generally accepted. But it would be a mistake to imagine them as watertight compartments with a sharp transition from one to the next. In fact, the earlier ones are integrated into the later ones, and in a sense provide the underpinning for them. The felt emotional states inculcated in childhood and early adolescence are quite healthy in themselves, and prevent us from doing many anti-social acts. It is because of this kind of psychological conditioning that we are freed from all kinds of irrational impulses. Because we don't have to battle with them and wonder on each occasion whether they are morally good or bad, we are free to devote our attention to more serious matters. Likewise, our conditioning in the area of conformity to law is a help insofar as we realize that there is simply not enough time in one lifetime to puzzle everything out for ourselves, so we take a lot of answers on the authority of others. But in the case of the morally mature person, this conditioning is not un-critically accepted. The conditioning which limits us in some areas of freedom is accepted for the sake of the greater freedom it provides in the more impor-tant matters of life. It frees us *from* irrational im-pulses, endless discussion and worry, and so frees us *for* the ordinary business of living.

The whole person

That the morally good person does not go around deceiving, assaulting or murdering people, however, is not simply the result of conditioning from without. On a certain level, the conditioning is a help. But the real reason is that he is a certain kind of person. It is because he has adopted a certain basic attitude, that his life has an overall pattern or orientation from the fact that he has accepted a set of values like respect for persons, truth, sincerity, love of God. When he consciously and freely acts against these, he expe-riences guilt, sin. Guilt for such a person is the con-sciousness of having acted against his conscience, of having sinned. The inconsistency between knowing and doing is felt as a break in his inner harmony. Since it is not just an abstract 'conscience' that makes the judgment, but the whole person of mind, will, body and emotions, the consciousness includes 'feelings' of shame, remorse, guilt. Though this feeling may be heightened by echoes from the past, it is still normal and healthy. It is morbid, unhealthy, irrational only when it is out of all proportion to the wrong done, or is unrelated to any real wrongdoing.

But, of course, few things in life are all or nothing, particularly in human affairs. Few people are at the top of the scale of moral maturity, whatever about the number who may be at the other end. Most people are at various points in between, and even within the same individual there can be varying mixtures of healthy and morbid, mature and childish. But it is important to be aware of the difference between the two, not to confuse neurotic guilt feelings with real moral guilt, or the super-ego with conscience.

Mature and immature

The super-ego is at work in a person who sees morality largely in terms of obedience to law or authority, who feels he constantly needs 'permissions' for things, and cannot act on his own responsibility. Such a person analyzes his moral behavior in isolated acts, with particular reference to the physical component, the quantified and easily measurable part. He is also very much concerned with the past, continually worrying about where he stands before God, afraid that God will tax him with some forgotten sin. He is particularly anxious in the area of sexuality, and is frequently plagued by scruples. He feels the need to be punished for his sins, and punishes himself even if only with his neurotic guilt feelings. The punishment can take various other forms. A circus performer used to end his nightly act by putting his head into the gaping jaws of a lion. The audience saw it as an act of daring, but he confessed to a friend that it terrified him to do it, but he did it each time as a punishment for a sin of his youth. The burden of guilt, imaginary and yet very real, can have almost cosmic proportions. A particularly sad case was that of the poor lady who was convinced that she was the cause of the Second World War because she concealed a minor sin in the confession prior to confirmation. The super-ego person's life is governed by rigid rules to which he feels bound. He seldom experiences a sense of freedom and shows little evidence of moral growth.

He has moments of elation after confession, but easily swings to deep depression.

The super-ego may also be *felt* by the morally mature person, but he is *not dominated* by it. He recognizes its presence, but has it under control. Such a person can respect law and authority, but his life is governed more by freely chosen values. His is a morality of responsibility rather than of permissions. He sees God as a loving Father interested in his growth and happiness, rather than as a hard taskmaster measuring guilt. He is more concerned about his basic attitudes and the overall pattern of his life than about isolated bits of behavior, though he is not careless about individual actions. He can accept responsibility for his failures and his sins. But he does not torment himself about them. He can forgive himself and feel loved and worthwhile, because he knows God forgives him. He believes that God loves him in spite of his sin, loves him for his own sake and not simply because he has earned such love by his good behavior. In repentence and trust, he can leave the past to God, live fully in the present and look confidently to the future.

Knowing his own limitations and weakness, he is constantly open to new information, new insights, and wants to grow in sensitivity and willingness to do good. He is ready to dialog with others and be corrected by them. His life is not tied to a rigid set of laws, but he is flexible, aware that growth is a slow process, that things take time. Though conscious of the danger of mediocrity and complacency, he does not get into a panic over the occasional lapse as long as he is doing his best. He knows that God listens to sentences rather than to isolated syllables.

From our discussion of the influence of the super-ego as distinct from mature conscience it would seem

to follow that some things considered as sins belong
more in the category of moral disease, that many of
the evil actions of everyday life, obsessive thoughts,
aggressiveness, etc. come more from psychological
complexes than from basic moral stance. Thus, ha-
bitual masturbation in people deeply committed to
God in prayer and service may not be so much sins as
simply unwanted victories of impulse over basic good
will and moral effort. The mature conscience will not
be complacent about or indifferent to such happen-
ings, but at the same time it will not react with the
panic of the super-ego. The morally mature person has
a calm approach to the problems of life, and whatever
the storms that trouble the surface of mind or emotion,
he can experience in the depth of his conscience the
peace that only God can give.

Felt experience needed

The fact that the super-ego can wreak such havoc in a
person's consciousness, that it can cripple one with
its burden of neurotic guilt, should make it clear that
there can be no instant cure. Merely *telling* a person
new facts may produce the illusion of an *informed*
conscience, but it will not develop a healthily *formed*
conscience. The formation of conscience is a lifelong
process involving the whole person, the feelings and
emotions and not merely the mind. The person operating with a childish, immature conscience, still under
the influence of the super-ego, certainly needs knowledge. He needs to be told of God's love and never-
ending forgiveness. He needs to be shaken free of the
rigidity of his views about obedience, law and authority. He could be enlightened about the influence
of authority figures in his early life, etc. But none
of this will do much good, no matter how loudly
preached or how often repeated, unless he also has

the *experience* of feeling worthwhile, of feeling that he is loved for his own sake and not for what he can do or contribute. He needs to experience the gospel as liberating Good News, setting him free personally, and not just as another message in words. He needs to experience a community of people who really care about him as a person, people who can mediate God's love to him in a way that can be felt.

Are we free?

If the super-ego person needs so much in order to be freed from the shackles of his neurotic guilt, it might well be asked, how many people in the world are really free? If they are not free, there can be no talk of sin. There is, in fact, a great deal of unfreedom in the world. There are limitations that come from one's physical make-up. For example, a connection has been found between the presence of an extra Y-chromosome in men or an extra X-chromosome in women and an exceptionally high incidence of juvenile delinquency, schizophrenia and homicidal behavior. There are internal pressures operating on the psyche, from mental retardation to severe emotional disturbances. There are people so blinded by racial or religious prejudice from their infancy and childhood that they are incapable of recognizing the human rights of the people they judge inferior. People who are socially and culturally deprived are less free than their more privileged neighbors. The vast majority of prisoners and mental patients come from the crowded ghettoes of our cities, from broken homes and inadequate parents. It would be a mistake, however, to judge that the majority of people in our prisons are sinners. Certainly, they are people paying a penalty for legal guilt, but only God can measure the degree, if any, of their moral guilt.

It could be concluded from these facts that man is not really free, that all his actions are in fact pre-determined by character, environment, upbringing and a host of physical and psychological factors. But against this, there is the firm conviction from the beginning of human history that man is accountable for his actions, that he is responsible for the choices he makes. By nature, man resists any kind of compulsion, and insists on his right to free action. Our awareness of freedom is also shown in the experience of conscience resisting temptation, going against the tide, saying No to convention and authority.

Taking these two sets of facts together, we conclude that human freedom is not absolute, but relative. Our actions are *conditioned* by the various forces mentioned above, but they are not *forced* by them. If an action is performed without any motive whatsoever, it is not deemed a human action, even though performed by a human being. It is the act of a person, but not acting *as* person. Human action, however, is always done for a *motive*, and the person decides which motives will determine his action. This is the experience of freedom. In the normal person this experience is accompanied by an awareness of *responsibility*. If one acts for a reason, one can be asked to give the reasons for one's decision and action, and one can be called to account for the consequences that flow from them.

Degrees of freedom

It is clear that among human beings there is a whole scale of different degrees of freedom, from the lowest to the highest. But it would be a mistake to picture the different degrees applying to different people and fail to realize that in each one of us there are large areas of unfreedom. Just as the divisions between

saint and sinner, believer and unbeliever are not
simply between groups of people, but cut through
each one of us, in the same way, the line between free
and unfree passes through each person. Each one of us
is a mixture of saint and sinner, free and unfree. These
pairs of terms are not put together simply for the sake
of literary apposition. There is a deep truth hidden in
the connection, namely that no human being is as free
as the saint, and that no one is as unfree as the sinner.
Sin is not only an abuse of freedom, but is itself a
danger to freedom and a limitation of freedom. In
what sense is this so?

Love and sin

St. Augustine said, 'Love God and do what you like.'
If I really love God with my whole heart, mind, soul
and strength, he becomes the center of my life, gives
meaning to it and to the whole of creation. My hope
is in him, my future is safe in his hands. He who cares
for the birds of the air and the lilies of the field will
see that I do not want. This gives me enormous freedom of mind, will and action. All my powers and
energies become available for others, for love, for
growth. By committing myself totally to God I seem to
lose myself, but this is the Christian paradox. Dying
to the sinful, self-centered self, I come alive to a better,
fuller, freer self. Losing my life in service and love,
I grow into a greater life of freedom and God's own
love.

But when I sin, the meaning goes out of my life, and
I have to search for a meaning of my own. When I put
God aside and self occupies the center, I become
aware of my needs, become preoccupied about meeting them, worry about the future and spend all my
energy building up security for myself, whether in
terms of wealth, power or reputation. In choosing to

put self first I narrow the range of my freedom. Since
I have decided to serve self, and the self has such
voracious needs, I am no longer free for others. Since
one of my most basic needs is to be loved, and I have
cut myself off from the love which gives me life and
meaning, I am no longer free to decide how I am going
to spend my life. The decision is already made for me
by the need of my nature. There is a never-ending
compulsion to pursue my own interests and desires,
and so more and more I concentrate on self. The nar-
rowing horizon lessens my options, so in a very real
sense my freedom is diminished, and I am really
enslaved.

Freedom of the children of God

When I choose God instead of self as the determining
factor in my life, I experience true freedom as a gift
from the source of all freedom. Paul speaks of the
'glorious freedom of the children of God' (Rom 8:21),
and pictures the whole of creation being set free from
its slavery to decay, groaning in its expectation. 'But
it is not just creation alone which groans; we who have
the Spirit as the first of God's gifts also groan within
ourselves, as we wait for God to make us his sons and
set our whole being free' (Rom 8:23). We wait to receive the gift. It has already been given in Christ, so
we really possess it, but we do not possess it fully,
so the battle between grace and sin, freedom and
unfreedom is fought out in the course of our lives.
We respond to God's gracious invitation, but it is not
a single Yes, an isolated decision. Rather it is a lifelong process of growing in his love and service, a
history of generosity and failures, of repentance and
repeated conversion.

All that has been said of the mature and immature
conscience, the various degrees of freedom and unfreedom, the multiplicity of influences at work in us,

and the continuing battle between grace and sin that is the pattern of our lives, should warn us against the false clarity and lust for certainty that constantly tempt us. Life is a messy business. There are many grey areas and there are mysteries we cannot fully understand. But it is in the bits and pieces of everyday that God comes to us, and he comes to each one of us where we are. He does not answer all our questions or solve our problems, but he gives us the ultimate meaning of it all and his grace provides us with the power to cope. By committing ourselves to him we gain a new freedom, but that freedom includes the possibility of saying No. We can sin, and we must accept our burden of guilt.

Guilt is real

Psychiatrists have much to tell us of neurotic guilt, so much in fact that there is a popular tendency to think that guilt itself is not a reality, but something purely subjective and imaginary. When we can point to authoritarian parents and the rigid conventions of society in the building up of the super-ego, there is a temptation to think that our guilt feelings are nothing but an over-active super-ego. A psycho-analyst, after hours of interviews, may dig up mountains of psychic garbage to probe the roots of the problem. As we have seen above, there is much we can learn from a study of the super-ego and the immature conscience. But it would be a pity if, whatever about the flaws in our early training and the psychic and social influences at work on our subconscious, we overlooked the definite and obvious possibility that we *feel* guilty because we *are* guilty. If our guilt feelings are a symptom of a personality disorder we may get help from a counsellor or psychiatrist. There is no need for repentance. But if our guilt is real sin, no amount of counselling or psychiatry is of any help.

What is needed in this case is repentance, conversion, atonement. The remedy is simple and easily available. God has given us the means to cope with sin. His forgiveness is there for the asking.

Sin is real

But even in the case of guilt as symptom of illness, there may be need for repentance and atonement. When the gospels quote Jesus associating illness and sin, perhaps they were not simply reflecting the simple, unsophisticated culture of the time. There can be a connection between the two insofar as human personality is all of a piece, and sin can have its effects on physical and mental health. I can nurse feelings of bitterness, resentment, anger or revenge until they come to possess my whole being. They literally take possession of me and dominate my life. Given the psycho-somatic unity of the human person, this experience can spill over and show up in one or other of the well-known psycho-somatic illnesses. A person in such a situation may benefit from the insights of a counsellor or psychiatrist, but he will not get to the root of his problem until he is reconciled with his brother. More than one psychiatrist has admitted: 'I envy priests their power to say: I absolve you from your sins'.

While it is not the business of therapists to take the place of a patient's conscience and make moral judgments for him, they ought to realize that it is good therapy to restore a person's sense of responsibility, insofar as possible. While it may interest the patient to be told that his present suffering and erratic behavior can be traced to faulty potty training or inadequate identification with the appropriate parent, this information may only aggravate the problem insofar as he feels that therefore he is no longer responsible for his actions and there is nothing he can do. Such a conviction may totally undermine his morale.

One of the deepest needs in human nature, apart from the need to love and be loved, is the need for respect. To tell a person, even by implication if not in so many words, that he is not really responsible, may give him momentary relief, but in the long run it is a failure to respect his personhood. It is much better to help him to accept his responsibility to whatever degree is possible, and to support him in his efforts to make amends. When real guilt has been discovered, even under a mountain of super-ego-produced fear and anxiety, it should be dealt with rationally when the patient is ready. Repentance and atonement can be real therapy, even though the neurotic guilt may still have to be dealt with by the professional therapist.

Love casts out fear

But some psychiatrists are coming to see that they are very limited in what they can do, that perhaps they would be better employed as researchers, theorists, or resource-people for counsellors. For one thing, they are far too few for the vast numbers of people needing help. Many of those few simply cannot afford the time that each patient would require, so they settle for a quick diagnosis and chemical prescription. They are not in a position to provide the affirming, supportive therapy that, in many cases, must continue for several years. Ordinary people with some skill and training in counselling who are prepared to really love the sufferer can provide more lasting help than the high-powered psychiatrist who

is only partly available. What the mentally and emotionally crippled people in our society need most of
all is someone who really *cares*, in a personal and
committed way, as Jean Vanier has proved. This is the
great challenge to our Christian community. Christ
promised the gift of healing to his church, so it ought
to be a place of healing. Looking at people weighed
down by such burdens of anxiety, fear and guilt, we
might ask where is the love that Jesus said would be
the hallmark of his followers? St. John tells us: 'There
is no fear in love; perfect love drives out all fear. So
then, love has not been made perfect in anyone who is
afraid, because fear has to do with punishment' (I Jn
4:18).

8

DOES GOD PUNISH SIN?

A major ingredient in neurotic guilt is the fear of punishment. The super-ego-ridden conscience tends to produce a super-ego type of religion which not only pictures God as a lawgiver laying down rigid rules, but fears him as a hard taskmaster. His all-seeing eye can penetrate one's actions to discover hidden motives, and his never-failing memory can recall forgotten or only half-confessed sins from the past. There is no avoiding his strict accounting, and though his justice may be tempered by mercy, it is still divine justice, reaching beyond the grave. Psychiatrists are familiar with the extreme forms which this irrational fear can take, and there are many people who suffer from it.

But even apart from the extremely neurotic cases, there are large numbers of good, conscientious people whose religion contains no small amount of fear. At least until very recently there were Catholics whose attendance at Sunday Mass was largely assured by their fear of mortal sin and eternal damnation. On the other hand, because many people no longer believe in hell they are less inclined to take sin seriously. An important element in the traditional notion of sin was not only that it was a transgression of God's law, but also that it was punishable by God. Can we still speak of punishment for sin? Are we still bound to believe in purgatory and hell?

Punishment in the bible

The biblical notion of sin certainly involved punishment. The author of Genesis speaks of God destroying

147

all of mankind except Noah and his family because sin had spread everywhere. The cities of Sodom and Gomorrah were likewise wiped out. Throughout the whole of the old testament God is pictured as reward- ing the good and punishing sinners. Since there was no belief in an afterlife for most of that period, the rewards and punishments were bestowed in this life. Health, long life and prosperity were counted as bless- ings from God for good behavior, while illness, defeat in battle or any other calamity was looked upon as an expression of God's judgment and anger. The picture that emerges is quite clear: God is really offended by sin, his wrath is aroused and he punishes the sinner. The new testament continues this picture. God's anger is manifest in the treatment given to the servant who showed no mercy (Mt 18:34), to the unfaithful servant (Mt 24:51), to those who killed the messengers inviting them to the wedding feast (Mt 22:7), and to the man without a wedding garment (Mt 22:13). It is evident in Jesus' condemnation of the unbelieving towns: 'You can be sure that on the Judgment Day God will show more mercy to Sodom than to you!' (Mt 20:24). It is clearest of all in his description of the final judgment: 'Away from me, you that are under God's curse! Away to the eternal fire which has been prepared for the devil and his angels!' (Mt 25:41).

Punishment in the church

The old testament people of God, the new testament Christian communities and the church through the centuries have all believed that God punishes sin. They believed in God as the just judge who would deal with each one according to his merits. The sinner upsets the order of justice, infringes rights, and he must be made to pay. Divine justice judges and con- demns him. While it was recognized that God would punish the sinner, the authorities in the community often took it upon themselves to mete out punishment in his name. Death, mutilation, excommunication were among the penalties inflicted by the community for various sins. Indeed, zeal for the rights and dignity of God led authorities to do the strangest things in his name and in his defense. The book of Leviticus commands the whole community to stone a blasphemer to death. The new testament recommends that he be 'handed over to satan'. The Inquisition gagged him and dragged him through the streets in disgrace. In seventeenth-century England, blasphemy was punished by boring a hole in the culprit's tongue. For a second offense, he would be stigmatized by having the letter B burned into his forehead, and for a third offense he would be sentenced to death without benefit of clergy, presumably so that he would go to hell, which he deserved. This notion of vindictive justice, that a sinner *deserves* punishment, and that it is imposed or inflicted from without, is still fairly common though gradually fading.

Throughout most of the old testament, God's reward or punishment was experienced this side of the grave. In this context, there was no solution to the problem of innocent suffering. The book of Job simply acknowledges the mystery, but cannot explain why so many of the wicked prosper and go unpunished, while Job the faithful has to suffer so much. But in the centuries immediately before Christ, belief in a real afterlife, as distinct from the shadowy underworld of Sheol, gradually began to take shape. The book of Daniel explicitly says: 'Many of those who have already died will live again: some will enjoy eternal life, and some will suffer eternal disgrace' (Dan 12:2). Paul told the Corinthians: 'For all of us must appear before Christ, to be judged by him. Each one will receive what he deserves, according to everything he

has done, good or bad, in his bodily life' (2 Cor 5:10).
The words of Jesus about Gehenna, the flames of hell
and the weeping and gnashing of teeth provided the
basis for the fire-and-brimstone preaching of later
centuries.

Catechism picture

The doctrine of hell and purgatory had quite a complicated theological history, but took definitive shape
during the middle ages, with no dogmatic additions
since. We have several times drawn attention to the
cultural conditioning of moral norms both in scripture
and in the documents of the church. Dogmatic statements about faith equally reflect the thought-
categories of the period in which they were formulated. This is even more true of their development
in catechisms and popular preaching through the ages,
and particularly so in the case of hell and purgatory.
Catechisms generally were a digest of theology textbooks, presenting an uncritical, undifferentiated
picture of 'the teaching of the church'. The short, con-
cise answers gave the impression of perfect clarity
and absolute certainty. The over-all picture was so
logical and consistent, with the various parts inter-
locking so perfectly, that people now fear that the
whole system will collapse because various items in
it no longer make sense. They need to be reassured
that the essentials of the faith remain intact and that
they have to be expressed in modern terms if they are
to carry conviction in today's world.

For the younger generation who may never have
seen such catechisms or heard such preaching, it may
be useful to recall the main points. Christian morality
is the effort to do God's will as manifested in scripture,
the teaching of the church and the dictates of one's
conscience. Deliberate failure is sin. This can be

mortal, which destroys the divine life of grace in the soul, or venial, which diminishes it but still leaves one in God's grace. To die in the state of mortal sin is to be excluded from the beatific vision of God in heaven, to be condemned to hell. Since the human soul is immortal, its punishment in hell will be eternal. Should one die in the state of grace, but not sufficiently pure to merit heven, purgatory would provide the necessary purification to enable one eventually to see God. In the forgiveness of sin, even when the guilt had been remitted, there remained a 'debt of temporal punishment' still to be paid. Should any of this remain outstanding at the moment of death, it could be taken care of in purgatory. The souls in purgatory were considered 'holy souls' because they were already sure of heaven (which is more than could be said of the living), and they could be helped in their expiation by the prayers of those still alive.

Purgatory and hell

This brief summary is hardly fair to the full teaching of the church, but it is an accurate enough description of the belief of the majority of the faithful. Popular imagination embroidered it with details not in the church's basic teaching. Many thought of purgatory as a kind of hell at a lower temperature or with the back-door open. Teachers were often quite eloquent in describing the particular torments that would afflict different kinds of sinner, both in hell and in purgatory. A widely-read pamphlet still current up to Vatican II spoke of a certain holy religious spending eighty years in purgatory for a minor imperfection and of others languishing there for years because they had no one to pray for them. In discussing the resurrection of the body, theologians explained that each person was judged individually at the moment of death, that his

'separated soul' went to its appropriate place of reward or punishment, and that his body would be
raised on the last day for a general judgment and
rejoin the soul in joy or torment.

Many people took all of this to be a description of
fact, ultimately revealed by God, and so were hesitant
to question it, in spite of the difficulties. With equal
simplicity they accepted accounts of visions by saints
who claimed to have seen souls falling into hell like
leaves in autumn. It is sad that there are people who
actually *like* to think like this, who feel that they are
defending God's justice when they take morbid
pleasure in such thoughts. For the saints, such a
picture caused intense sadness and spurred them to
greater penance and prayer. In actual fact, the official
teaching of the church is quite sober. It says nothing
whatever about the number of people in hell. Indeed,
there is no statement to commit us to believing that
anybody is there, even Judas. All that the church in
its official statements is committed to on the subject
is: that hell exists as the consequence of final personal
separation from God, that it begins immediately after
death, and that it lasts forever. Anything beyond that
is guesswork and theological opinion.

The doctrine of purgatory is an essential element in
Christian faith. But official teaching simply says
that there is a purification for all who die truly penitent in the love of God before satisfying for their
sins through worthy acts of penance. It adds that they
can be helped by the prayers of the faithful, and especially by the sacrifice of the Mass. Nothing more.
There is no official statement of the church obliging
us to believe anything about the nature of the purification or its duration. Whether purgatory is a place,
a state or simply a process is not mentioned, nor do we
have to believe in fire or specific torments. Any discussion of hell or purgatory should begin with the

sober statements of the official teaching of the church, and carefully distinguish this from further developments. Given the human thirst for knowledge, man's unrestricted desire to know, it is natural that the basic truths be teased out for further detail, that we try to make them meaningful in our current culture. But we must be careful not to ask the wrong questions, not to expect more than is possible, or indeed more than is necessary.

New approach

In an earlier chapter we made reference to the fact that the book of Genesis tells us nothing about what happened at the beginning of time, but gives us the ultimate and therefore religious meaning of what is happening all the time. We have long since stopped asking the bible and the teaching church for answers to scientific questions about the shaping of the universe or the age of man. It took quite a while, and no small amount of suffering and frustration, for this to be recognized by the authorities in the church. It is time people realized that the same principle applies at the other end of man's history, both personal and cosmic. Biblical statements and church teaching on purgatory and hell are not meant as advance coverage on the details of future life. They are not so much statements from the final chapter in the history of salvation as basic truths which help us to a better understanding of our present life and of the seriousness of the struggle between grace and sin, freedom and unfreedom. It is a trivialization of heaven, hell and purgatory to think of them simply and solely as future states, as reward and punishment for present behavior.

It is true that Jesus himself used the language of reward and punishment: 'Well done, good and faithful

servant . . .' and 'Depart from me, you cursed ones.'
He could hardly do otherwise than use the language of
his time. But the idea of God sitting in judgment at
the end of the race seems to drag him down to our level,
and the very concept of vindictive justice is alien to
the notion of a God who is infinite love and wills the
salvation of all men. It can be a frightening thing,
frightening in the sense of awesome, to fall into the
hands of the living God, and reverential fear is the
beginning of wisdom. But God wants our love, and
this will not come from fear. St. John reminds us that
fear has to do with punishment, but 'perfect love
drives out all fear' (I Jn 4:18). Too much in our understanding of the punishment for sin came from our
experience of penal laws in civil society. The social
element in sin, the harm done to others, calls for
compensation or restitution, but it is difficult to
imagine God gaining anything by punishing us for
the sake of his justice. Just as we found a meaningful
way of understanding God's will without thinking of a
law extrinsically imposed, so we can speak meaningful of punishment for sin without picturing God
inflicting punishment from without.

Judgment not God's condemnation

While allowing for the use of metaphor in the bible
and in Christian tradition, it would be wrong to dismiss references to 'God's anger' as mere anthropo-
morphism, speaking of God in human terms. Behind
such phrases is the firm belief that God is a personal
being who is not indifferent to our behavior, that he
is the All-Holy, that he is a loving Father who really
cares and is concerned about our welfare. All references to the anger and judgment of God in both old
and new testaments, however, need to be balanced
against the emphasis on God's love. The key to a more

satisfactory understanding of punishment for sin is to be found in the words of Jesus himself: 'If anyone hears my message and does not obey it, I will not judge him. I came, not to judge the world, but to save it. Whoever rejects me and does not accept my message has one who will judge him. The words I have spoken will be his judge on the last day!' (Jn 12:47-48). There is no need for a judgment by God extrinsically decreed, nor for punishment inflicted from without. Man is continually being called to judgment, continually being faced with the challenge of Jesus and his words. He cannot be neutral. He must decide whether he will serve God or Mammon. His own decision is his judgment. It is his own act, and punishment is simply the inevitable and natural consequence of sin. It occurs in the very moment of sin and continues throughout the state of sinfulness.

Sin its own punishment

Sin does bring punishment, therefore, but from within itself, in terms of alienation and disintegration. The sinner is no longer the integrated, Christ-centered person God invites him to be, the person growing in love as he reaches out more and more to others, but a disintegrated person, divided within himself, cut off from his true self, from others, from the world about him, and from God. This, of course, refers to the state of mortal sinfulness, which excludes God and enthrones self at the center of life. In this state, as we saw in the last chapter, man still has freedom of choice, but the range of his freedom is radically diminished, and on the deepest level he is enslaved to self. Having rejected God's love, the sinner loses his own power to love, though he may keep its appearances. If his life is really dominated by self instead of God, he will be incapable of loving others for their own sake. They will be desired, exploited or dominated as objects for his own selfish interests. Since a basic need of our nature is the need to love and be loved, the sinner's inability to love is a loss at the most funda-mental level of his being. He is not only a stranger to himself, but is estranged from his fellowmen, and no matter how much he surrounds himself with com-pany, his heart experiences a profound loneliness. The very presence of others only aggravates the sear-ing pain of his utter aloneness. The sinner is the only one who can echo with conviction Sartre's famous words: 'Hell is other people'.

Hell begins on earth

It is a mistake to picture hell simply as a punishment coming at the end of life, a sudden shock of a new experience. Hell after death is simply the continuation and the logical consequence of a selfish, sinful pattern of life, the definitive state of mortal sinfulness. To experience the basic need for love and yet find it totally and continually frustrated is to be in hell already in this life, and to have it go on endlessly is worse than the hell-fire of medieval theology. Sartre's play *Huis Clos* is a brilliant imaginative picture of what hell may be like. The three characters are pre-sented as having just died. They are in hell, pictured as a drab drawing-room without windows or mirrors, and it is clear that they have become the kind of people they are because of the way they lived. They are pathetically reaching out to each other looking for sympathy, understanding and love, but each is so preoccupied with self, so totally locked up in self, that there is no love to give, and yet they cannot give up the effort, so there is the hell of constant striving and longing continually frustrated. In this kind of approach, hell is a state of mental anguish prepared for and begun in this life, but reaching a point of no return in death when the sinner says a total and definitive No to God. If hell is prison, there is no greater hell than to be locked up within oneself when that self has become infinitely small through rejection of God.

Some theologians would go so far as to say that since sin is negative selfishness, we can, by the way we live, become so turned in on self and so totally negative, that we have nothing to carry over into eternity, that we simply disappear or cease to exist as persons. Growth in Christ and living for others, on the other hand, is a positive reality enabling us to live on forever in the intimacy of God's family. Then we can love fully without the barriers that at present tend to keep us apart.

There is no need to picture judgment at death in terms of God searching his account books to see whether we have a credit or debit balance. He has only to look at us to know whether we belong with him. If we have lived the Christ-life (known explicitly or only implicitly), reaching out in genuine care and concern for others, he sees the image of Christ in us and recognizes us as his children. Heaven means being at home with God who is infinite love. It begins in this life insofar as to live the Christ-life is to increase our capacity for love, to grow in the likeness of Christ, to relate to God as our Father.

This approach is beautifully put by James Michener in *The Fires of Spring:*

'Then from a side bench a man in gray rose and began to speak. Neither David nor Marcia knew this Quaker, nor would they ever know his name, but his words fell over the ugly architecture of their past like snow upon the buildings of Washington Square. He said: 'The most misleading concept in religion is that of the recording angel. I cannot believe that God remembers or cares to remember a single incident of our lives. I am the recording angel. My spirit and my body are the record. My good deeds show in me, and my wrong deeds can never be hidden. My spirit either grows to fullness or declines to nothing. God has no need of recording devices. We must not think of him as a vengeful or shopkeeping dictograph. He has created a better instrument than a strip of all-recording film. He has made me. He needs only look to me, and all is recorded.

'Therefore we must conclude that we retain the privilege of erasing past mistakes. Sometimes I think we Quakers do not attend carefully enough to the teachings of the Catholic Church. I refer especially to their doctrine of final salvation. I know it is repugnant for some Friends to contemplate a totally evil man's being saved in the last gasp of life, but if what I have just said about God's establishing us as his immortal recording devices is true, I for one believe this to be possible.' (p. 445, London, 1949).

Fear of hell

All our talk of future existence, of course, it simply guesswork and very much an over-simplification. There are difficult philosophical and theological problems about the details of life after death and the resurrection of the body. Our belief in bodily resurrection stresses the essential fact of continuity and personal survival, but the church is in no way committed to any particular theological opinion about the details. Our faith does not oblige us to believe that anyone is actually in the state of hell as final, irrevocable separation from God. It does require us to believe that God who is all-powerful and infinite love wills all men to be saved, but that man is capable of rejecting God's love. Hell in this sense is a real possibility for each and every one of us. To fear it is not to be terrified by an unchristian avenging God waiting to punish us, but to be conscious of the seriousness of life, to be concerned and awed by the fact that we can sinfully refuse God's gift of love, and to be constantly reminded of the need for repentance and conversion.

Purgatory today

Heaven and hell are not simply state of life after death, but realities prepared for and already begun this side of the grave, eschatological conditions with all the tension of the 'here and now' but 'not yet' about them. In the same way, *purgatory* as a purifying process has its beginnings here on earth. As we have just seen, the punishment for sin, begun even in this life, is really the effect of sin itself on our being. Even apart from the consequences our sin may have for others, injuring their person, their property or their reputation, poisoning the moral climate of the community or damaging the physical environment, all sin has an effect on ourselves. Apart from the harm particular sins may do to our health, every sin leaves its mark, deep or shallow, on our personality, making us the kind of person we are. Since all sin is selfishness, every sinful decision increases the selfish streak in our nature. It affects our relationship with God and neighbor, and disrupts our inner harmony.

When we repent and receive God's forgiveness, we are healed by his grace at the core of our being. It is possible that our repentance and conversion will be a dramatic experience, turning us inside out and shaking us to the foundations. But it is seldom like that. It is not often, if ever, that we are capable of taking the whole of ourselves into a single act. Our conversion is a reorientation of our life back to God, but it takes time for this to be worked out fully so that it penetrates all areas of our lives, all levels of our heart. The sin itself is forgiven and is now no more, but its effects (which are not sins) still need to be dealt with. Repentance is more than just sorrow for sin. To be genuine, it must involve atonement, and this means restoring 'at-oneness' between ourselves and God (by prayer and prayerful love of neighbor), between ourselves and our neighbor (by restitution and loving service), and within ourselves (by mortification, discipline, self-control). It should be obvious that these are not three water-tight compartments that can be taken care of in isolation. Work in any one area will not be genuine unless it reaches over into the others. Even prayer can be an escape, and it is an illusion unless it also finds expression in service.

Purifying process

What all this means is that repentance is not just a decision, but also a process that takes time, that must reach into the different levels of our being. God's forgiveness heals the root of our problem, transforms us into new creatures, but he expects us to cooperate with his grace in healing the effects of sin. This is what penance is all about. Should death intervene before the process is complete, the remainder is taken care of by what we call *purgatory*. This is a purification after death enabling us to become whole persons, purged of the last traces of selfishness, and ready to enjoy the happiness of heaven. There is no need to think of it as a place in which people have to spend time until they are released. Much less should we picture it as a prison with half-forgotten cells, requiring frantic prayers for 'the most abandoned souls in purgatory'.

We are free to think of it as a process of purfication which may well be instantaneous, occurring in the very instant of death and the vision of God. It can be thought of as a painful release from everything opposed to God, a bringing together and maturing of all that is incomplete and unfinished in us. To come into the blinding light of God's infinite love with the consciousness of our own lack of love, to meet our heavenly Father with the awareness that our spirit of sonship has not yet penetrated to all levels of our heart, is to suffer intense pain. To look into the eyes of love in this state can be a searing agony, but it is a purifying, transforming one, and in that same instant it is changed into the joy of ecstasy. Differences between the experiences of individuals could well be different degrees of intensity depending on the spiritual state of each. People undergoing such a painful, but purifying experience can be helped by our prayers, not in the sense of having others pay the fine for their release, but in the sense that they are supported by the solidarity of the communion of saints. Our faith in purgatory is not helped by stories of deceased priests appearing to friends to appeal for certain forgotten Masses to be celebrated so that they can be released from their pain. God is not honored when we see him as a super-accountant busy with heavenly book-keeping. We should pray for our deceased and remember them particularly in the great sacrament of unity which is the eucharistic offering of the Mass, but there is no need to worry about the measuring or the mechanics of its efficacy.

The future is here

Christian faith will always be curious to know the details of the great truths, so we will continue to search for ways of making them meaningful in each new age. Whichever theories of heaven, hell and purgatory we find most helpful, we need to remember that they are only theories, and must be constantly checked against the basic teaching of the church, however bare and sober this may seem to be.

The mystics often speak of the acceptance of a certain degree of ignorance as a mark of wisdom. The reminder is especially necessary in our present context. We know nothing of the details of life after death, and perhaps it is just as well. Faith has to do with the meaning of life rather than with the geography or furniture of heaven and hell. Preoccupation with future states could distract us from the business of everyday living and let us forget that the realities of heaven and hell begin here on earth. Jesus came, as he tells us, that we 'might have life, life in all its fullness' (Jn 10:10), not simply as a future reward, but as a here and now possession. When we look forward to the fullness of that life beyond the limitations of our present existence, there is no need to fear, because the God we meet is not the God who punishes, but the loving and faithful God who wants all men to be saved. It is not quite true that God punishes sin, but sin is its own punishment. What we need to fear is our own sinfulness, what it can do to us, and most of all our refusal to repent, to be converted, and to accept the gift of God's forgiveness.

9

GOD'S GIFT OF FORGIVENESS

Whatever about the therapy required to deal with neurotic guilt, there is a sure-fire remedy available for real guilt and sin, namely repentance, atonement and forgiveness. On the level of human relationships there is a sense of new life and fresh start when an apology has been accepted and the broken strands of love brought together again. But when the forgiveness comes through the sacramental action of the church, backed by the authority and power of Jesus himself, it can bring a peace not of this world. Christians through the centuries have experienced sacramental confession as a real safety-valve for their accumulated burden of guilt, and received the words of absolution as a healing balm for mind and heart. But, like so many other elements in the life of the church, our experience of God's forgiveness in the sacrament of penance had its own historical development through the centuries. Christ empowered his church to forgive sins in his name, but it took over a thousand years for the sacrament to develop into the form in which we know it today. Most people would be surprised to hear that St. Augustine never went to confession, and that for centuries the saintly bishops of Gaul preached that one should *do* penance, but go to confession only on one's deathbed.

It would be a mistake to imagine that we have nothing to learn from the past, or to think that developments in the church have always been for the best because they were directly under the guidance of the Holy Spirit. In fact, history is there to show that Christ's promise of being with his church until the end of time is no guarantee against its making mistakes. The church is not only a community of sinners needing constant reform and continual conversion, but a human family subject to the ordinary laws of human growth. This growth has its share of groping and stumbling, experimenting and learning. It brings into the future not only its successes, but also the traces of some of its less happy experiences and even its mistakes. Thus, our present understanding and practice of the sacrament of penance is not all that it could be. The new rites of celebration are an attempt to improve it, but they will have little effect unless the faithful (including bishops and priests) have a proper understanding of sin, repentance, conversion, reconciliation, penance and the sacramental celebration of God's forgiveness. Such an understanding, of course, will be colored by one's notion of God, of the church and of sacraments in general.

Problems

Too many people still have a taboo notion of morality and a magical idea of the sacraments. The impression is still abroad that only in confession are sins *really* forgiven; an act of perfect contrition is supposed to achieve the same result, but one needs to be almost a saint to make one, in which case it would not be needed in the first place. Some confessors are still preaching the 'gas-station' concept of grace; one can never get enough of a good thing, and frequent confession keeps one continually 'topped up'. Few people see any intimate connection between the sacrament of penance and the penitential elements of prayer, fasting and almsgiving involved in conversion.

Many use the sacrament simply as a 'guilt-shedding' process with little real experience of reconciliation or spiritual growth. Some confess the same 'laundry-list' each time and yet are dissatisfied because it does not enable them to cope with all the sinfulness they are conscious of. The present practice of private confession cannot deal with communal responsibility for sinful structures or a sinful climate of opinion. Others are so concerned about law and measurement that their confession leaves large areas of morality untouched because there are no specific laws or they are not easily measured. Since the *Humanae Vitae* debate, many people who feel free in conscience to practice contraception nevertheless feel guilty about not mentioning it in confession. Those who do confess it 'shop around' for a sympathetic priest, and they feel the variety of views and attitudes confusing. They wonder about the priest's precise role as confessor.

Many people think of sin simply as an offense against God, and see the priest as his representative, so that the church as community is almost totally bypassed both in the confession and in the absolution. Present practice can foster an individualistic piety. Besides, the idea of penance as reconciliation is obscured by equating obligatory and devotional confession, since it is difficult to speak of real reconciliation with the church in the case of minor daily sins. Although the Council of Trent's demand for integral confession of sins according to number and kind referred only to mortal sins, children were trained to think of it as applying to all sins, so that many adults still engage in a frantic search for everything they can possibly think of, and their almost neurotic preoccupation with self sometimes blots out all awareness of the tremendous gift that is God's forgiveness. Likewise, too much emphasis on the priest's role as judge can give the impression of a criminal court where every last ounce of guilt must be accurately measured and ultimately paid for.

Forgotten truths

Even before we look to the new rites, there are some 'forgotten truths' about the sacrament of reconciliation that we need to be reminded of: the theological nature of sin; a more nuanced presentation of the distinction between sins, including the dropping of the over-simplified 'mortal-venial' division; the importance of the 'time' or 'process' element in both sin and reconciliation, so that confession is simply the sacramental moment in a process of repentance; the fact that there are various forms of penance (ordinary, everyday ones and liturgical ones, sacramental and non-sacramental); that the obligation of private confession applies only to those who are conscious of sin which is *subjectively* serious; that confession of necessity and confession of devotion ought to be clearly distinguished; that grace and spiritual benefit are not increased in mathematical proportion to the frequency of confession; that the eucharist itself has a propitiatory value, so that for those properly disposed it can bring the grace of forgiveness.

If these points are properly understood, a reduction in the numbers approaching the sacrament or less frequency of individual confession need not cause alarm. There may be a danger that some will look to communal celebrations for a kind of cheap grace, a too-easy forgiveness, but even at present one could well wonder about the meaningfulness of many weekly confessions. A situation that ought to raise questions is the fact that large numbers of men attend Sunday Mass faithfully but hardly ever receive communion. Is this a problem of conscience, a fear of confession, or a lack of appreciation of the full meaning of the eucharist?

Ordinary means of penance

In speaking of God's forgiveness, the impression should not be created that the sacrament of penance is the *only* means, or indeed the only safe or sure way of receiving it. People need to be told of the importance and efficacy of the ordinary, everyday means of reconciliation. We saw that sin weakens or destroys our relationship with God, alienates us from our fellowmen, and disrupts the inner harmony of our lives. Penance is not just paying a fine for wrongdoing, accepting punishment inflicted by a vengeful God. Rather, it is a reversal of the sinful process that turned us from God and neighbor and left us divided within ourselves. We are reconciled to God by prayer, particularly the Our Father. If we can say this prayer with our whole being, really mean every word of it and try to live the attitude it reflects, then we are once more children of God. Our reconciliation with each other can be brought about by restitution where necessary, and by almsgiving, not merely the giving of money, but of our time, talent, energy, sympathy, in a word, by our giving of ourselves. We can be healed within ourselves from our weakness and self-indulgence through fasting and self-denial. Traditionally, these three: prayer, almsgiving and fasting, are the the main forms of penance.

The new testament gives special emphasis to mutual pardon as a necessary condition for divine forgiveness, and later tradition singled out the Our Father and holy communion as means of reconciliation. Daily work can have a penitential value. The penalty mentioned in the Genesis account of sin: 'You will have to work hard and sweat to make the soil produce anything' (3:19), could be seen not simply

as a result of sin, its punishment, but also as a means
of reconciliation. Our daily work can associate us
with God's own creativity in improving the world,
enable us to cooperate with others and give us a sense
of fulfillment and inner peace. The whole Christian
life should be a spiritual sacrifice offered for sin. It
is a pity that these ordinary, everyday means of
pardon have been so neglected in the last few centuries, as though confession were the only way. Without minimizing the value or usefulness of confessions
of devotion, we need to realize that God's grace and
pardon come to us through the events of daily life.
These ordinary means of pardon are always available,
and they can be a safeguard against the formalism
of mere good intentions and the too easy 'three Hail
Mary's' so often handed out for sacramental penance.

Penance and confession

If sin is a process brought about by and given expression in concrete actions, the same is true of repentance; it is a process involving time. Like the lost son
in Christ's parable, the sinner 'comes to his senses',
realizes his tragic situation and repents. At the first
genuine turning towards God, the heavenly Father
reaches out in forgiveness, and the wandering son is
once more at home. On God's part, the act of forgiveness is instantaneous and pure gift, not an earned
reward. But on the sinner's part, this return to God's
friendship is only the beginning of a process. It will
take time to repair the harm done to others and to let
conversion have its full effect on mind, will and emotions. This is the area of asceticism, of prayer, almsgiving and penance. In the case of more serious sins,
the sinner must be so disposed that he is willing, at an
appropriate time, to confess these sins to a priest.
To refuse to be confronted with the incidents which

broke his relationship with God calls into question the sincerity of his repentance.

The reason for confession as part of the process of reconciliation is that sin is never a purely private affair. Even our most secret sins affect our brethren in the community, and when we sin grievously we cut ourselves off not only from Christ, but from his mystical body, the community of his followers. For repentance to be genuine, therefore, it must be not merely a turning back to God, but a firm desire to be reconciled with the community. Private confession to the person offended may reconcile one to that particular person, and where possible this ought to be done. But reconciliation with the church as such can only be effected through bishop or priest empowered to act on behalf of the community. It is this official reconciliation with the community which has been singled out by the church as the sacramental moment in the process of repentance and forgiveness. This is the *sacrament*. In this encounter between priest and penitent the mystery and gift of God's forgiveness reaches a focal point of special intensity and meaning. Reconciliation with the community is the outward sign of reconciliation with God, and the absolution given by the priest is the concrete expression of God's forgiveness.

It is in this wider context of penance, the penitential process and community, that we should consider the sacrament. Keeping this background in mind may provide a safeguard against slot-machine absolutions and a magical approach to confession. By taking some of the emphasis off the listing of sins it may help people towards a more Christian notion of the God of infinite love, especially those people who continually confess doubtful sins or incidents from their 'past life'. One gets the impression that they confess these 'just in case' God might have something on them,

fearing that God might present them at judgment day
with a list of sins they had somehow committed without being aware of it. They use confession almost to
insure themselves against God. Many of these attitudes owe their origin to distorted notions or exaggerated emphases on different aspects of the sacrament in the course of its history.

New testament

It would be naive to imagine that the sacrament as we
know it came directly from Christ himself. In its
modern form it is nowhere to be found in the new
testament, but penance and the forgiveness of sins
are at the very center of the preaching of Jesus. He
began his ministry with the call to 'repent and believe
the gospel' and he took leave of his disciples with the
command that 'in his name the message about repentance and the forgiveness of sins must be preached to
all nations' (Lk 24:47). Jesus himself forgave sins
(Mk 2:2-12; Lk 7:36-50), and he expressly entrusted
to this church disciplinary power over believers who
fall into sin (Mt 18:15-17). After a fruitless private
monition or before two witnesses, the sinner is to be
denounced to the church, and, if he will not accept
correction he is to be treated as the heathen and the
publican, i.e. to be excommunicated. In Jn 20:22-23,
he told his disciples: 'Receive the Holy Spirit. If you
forgive people's sins, they are forgiven; if you do not
forgive them, they are not forgiven'.

Penance plays an important part in the epistles of
Paul, and he makes clear that the church's decisions
with regard to a sinner have supratemporal consequences. James and John speak of the universality of
sin and of its power, but they both emphasize that
divine forgiveness is universal, that even the gravest
sinner can count on forgiveness. The only exception
is the 'sin against the Holy Spirit', which would seem

to be the sin of final impenitence, the radical closing in on self that makes the sinner incapable of responding to grace.

Early centuries

In the first few centuries it was left to the bishop in each area to detemine the way in which the gospel principles of forgiveness would be implemented. Gradually set forms of administration took shape. A sinner could go to a spiritual counsellor to confess secret grave sins, and the counsellor would decide whether the sins were grave enough to warrant public penance, but he did not give absolution. This came after the penance was completed, and was a solemn reconciliation, usually on Holy Thursday. The public penances became quite harsh, including fasting and sexual abstinence, lasting for years, sometimes for life. The severity of these penances, especially the prohibition of the use of marriage for so many years, resulted in the postponement of penance for as long as possible, and a stage was reached when the church actually forbade the admission of young people to penance lest they be unable to continue it. More and more it became simply a preparation for death. The church became a victim to its own rigidity, so that for centuries no sacraments at all were available for the long years of a man's life when sins were most frequent.

So fixed was this attitude that a council of bishops at Toledo in 589 condemned repeated confession as an abuse. But the practice was already fairly widespread, coming from the Celtic churches, and by the seventh century frequent confession was common. In Ireland, penance was private, consisting in confession, the acceptance of the penance prescribed by the priest, and finally reconciliation. Many penitents did not return for reconciliation, so gradually the practice developed of granting absolution at the time of confession and the penance was done afterwards. This eventually became the common practice of the church.

To help confessors in the administration of the sacrament, the Irish church invented the so-called *penitential books*, which listed the penances for various types of sins, graded according to severity, hence called *tarrif* penances. Prayer, fasting, abstitence from marital intercourse, pilgrimage or exile were all imposed. Some were for life, others for years, from thirty down to one. For lighter sins: forty days down to one day. Seven days fasting was the penalty for drunkenness, one day for immoderate eating. A long penance could be exchanged for a shorter one of greater intensity. This kind of substitution was often necessary because several lifetimes would not be sufficient to carry out the accumulated burden of penance in some cases.

Of course these penances must be judged against the general harshness of life in those centuries. The penitential books stressed the need for contrition and conversion, and in spite of the emphasis on penitential works, the ecclesiastical and sacramental aspect of penance was quite clear. The obligation of annual confession was laid down by the 4th Lateran Council in 1215, which also imposed the strictest secrecy on the confessor. The Council of Trent added the obligation of integrity, that is, that all mortal sins be confessed in detail according to number and kind. In 1576 St. Charles Borromeo decreed that every church was to have a confessional box, a step which completed the privatization of the sacrament.

Confession and communion

Until the beginning of this century the vast majority of people rarely received communion. In 506 the

Council of Agdes imposed the obligation of communion three times a year (Christmas, Easter and Pentecost), but in 1215 the universal law for the church decreed simply 'at least at Easter'. There were two traditions with regard to the need for confession. According to one, the eucharist itself included forgiveness, hence the penitential rite at the beginning of the celebration (general confession of sinfulness and a form of absolution), but after the 4th Lateran Council more and more theologians insisted on private confession of grave sins as a requirement for the reception of communion.

Inevitably, confession came to be seen as preparation for communion, so that when Pius X in 1905 recommended frequent and even daily communion, the practice of weekly or monthly confession quickly followed. This is the pattern most of today's Catholics are familiar with. But the pattern has dramatically broken up in the last few years. Some of the reasons for dissatisfaction with the recent tradition have already been mentioned. We need to ask: what can be learned from the history of the sacrament, even in the brief outline we have just glimpsed? For one thing, it might relativize some of the elements we have tended to look on as absolutes, and at least it can shake us out of the rigidity that so often stifles development.

Various forms

The sacrament took many forms down through the centuries, and some of them continued side by side for years. Jesus spent much of his time with sinners and outcasts and had harsh words for the self-righteous religious establishment. He forgave sin and empowered the community of his followers to do the same, but he did not spell out the ways in which it was to be done. The church, responding to people's need for forgiveness, created new forms of penance

as they were needed to meet the needs and understanding of a particular age. In the first two centuries
the church consisted of small, closely-knit communities centered on the weekly eucharist. Christians
confessed to one another, admonished one another,
forgave each other. For serious sin, a brother would
be excluded, put out of the community, but his brethren continued to pray for him until he could return.
The community felt responsible for the sinner. When
it was feared that reconciliation was becoming too
easy and Christians might grow lax, the practice of
public penance was introduced. This served its purpose for a while, but then hardened to the point where
pardon was not available until immediately before
death.

The good sense of the community gradually moved
away from this extreme and developed private penance and more frequent confession. For the convenience of the faithful, the order of penance and absolution was inverted so that forgiveness was granted
before the penance was carried out. But with the loss
of community awareness, the role of the confessor
increased; he was spiritual father, teacher, physician
and judge. He was seen as God's representative, and
sin was more and more considered simply as a personal breaking of God's law. Private and frequent
confession did wonders for the spiritual life of the
faithful, and people traveled miles to avail of holy
confessors like the Cure of Ars, but the practice also
encouraged an individualistic piety. The detailed
listing of sins and the minute examination of degrees
of guilt often gave rise to scruples, and on the other
hand it totally ignored the social dimension of sin.

New rites

The new legislation (1974) on the sacrament of reconciliation allows for four types of celebration: 1)

individual confession and absolution, 2) individual confession and absolution fitted in between communal preparation and thanksgiving, 3) communal penitential services to promote a spirit of repentance, but which do not forgive serious sin, and 4) general confession of sinfulness, followed by general absolution, but with the obligation to confess privately at a later date. This last form is restricted to quite exceptional circumstances, which, in the opinion of many bishops, are not likely to arise outside of some missionary countries.

These new rites are an attempt to recapture some of the best insights of the past. The sacrament is described as *reconciliation* rather than just *confession*. Some prominence is given to sacred scripture, emphasizing its healing power as well as the fact that it calls us to judgment. Communal celebrations allow for a homily and also enable the community to acknowledge responsibility for the general sinfulness of society. They bring home the fact that we are a community of sinners needing God's healing and pardon. However, many theologians cannot see why actual forgiveness is still restricted to private confession except on occasions so rare as to make them not worth counting. They maintain that sins are indeed forgiven in the third form of celebration, without private confession and individual absolution. This is not necessarily 'cheap grace', because most people who have had this experience also use and appreciate private confession, and for many who had not been to confession for years it was the step that helped them to return. The second form, combining communal and individual, is clumsy and impractical except for well-organized, small groups with no shortage of confessors.

The new rites are an attempt to revitalize the sacrament, but the restrictive way in which they are interpreted means that they will make it just a little more meaningful, and then only for the devout. They are not going to work wonders. They will make little difference to large numbers who have real difficulty with traditional confession practice. One wonders if the words of Jesus about leaving the ninety-nine and going after the one lost sheep have any application in this context. Perhaps the new legislation is simply a holding operation, a slow, tiny step in the direction of a better understanding of the sacrament, which will evolve further when people are ready. But much more needs to be done to help people towards not only an understanding, but an actual experience of the mystery and gift of God's forgiveness.

Need for balance

It would be a pity to encourage one form of penance at the expense of the others, or to see the sacrament in isolation from the whole process of reconciliation. Both communal and private celebrations of the sacrament are necessary and should complement each other. We need to trust people a little more, and the only way to trust them is to actually *trust* them. St. Paul tells to examine *ourselves* (I Cor 11:28). Much more could be left to the personal responsibility of individuals with regard to self-examination and self-discipline. They could decide which forms are more appropriate for them at any given time. On the other hand, the faithful have a right to expect guidance and help from the church. The two need to be kept in balance.

It is understandable that authorities in the church should feel the weight of their responsibility before God for the spiritual welfare of those entrusted to their guidance. They also feel responsible for sacred scripture, the sacraments and for the things of God in general, which they must safeguard and protect.

But occasionally they give the impression that they are defending God, in which case it needs to be asked whether it is really God or a particular notion of God that is being defended.

History shows how often the church tied itself into a straight-jacket of immobility with too much legislation, how laws intended to bring people closer to God actually kept them at a distance from him. Jesus pointed out that the sabbath was made for man, and not vice versa. In the same way, theologians constantly remind us that the sacraments are for the faithful, not the other way round. But it is not clear how far this is accepted in practice. Most of the talk about new forms of the sacrament of reconciliation is restricted to the clergy. The faithful have heard about 'new rites', but over ninety per cent of them have not the faintest idea of what the discussion is all about. This is the context in which God's forgiveness has to be preached.

Forgiveness God's gift

Reference has already been made to the 'forgotten truths' about penance that need to be recalled. Perhaps the greatest and most forgotten truth of all is that God's forgiveness is sheer gift, unearned, unmerited. In our concern to see that God is not mocked or even slighted, we may have lost our perspective. Though we speak of the gift of his forgiveness, most people feel that they must earn it, be worthy of it, that it comes only after they have done their penance, paid their fine. But this is not the impression we get from Jesus. Both in his own ministry of forgiveness and in his preaching he makes it clear that the initiative comes from God, that forgiveness is the gift of his love, and that the works of penance are the result of it, not the condition for its granting. This is particularly evident in his words to Simon the Pharisee about the sinful woman: 'I tell you, the great love she has shown proves that her many sins have been forgiven' (Lk 7:47). She was not forgiven because of her great love, but her love was the effect of forgiveness.

The parable of the lost son (Lk 14:11-32) is the classical sermon on God's mercy, but how many people appreciate it fully? The younger son is the average sinner, independent, wanting to go his own way, to cut loose from home and community. When 'at last he came to his senses', he decided to return to his father with the confession: 'I have sinned against God and against you'. But the original motive for his change of heart was selfish enough: the contrast between the comfort of home and his own sad situation. The father did not wait for him to prove his worthiness. He did not give him a trial period as slave, then hired worker, before accepting him again as his son. He had never ceased loving him. His love respected the young man's decision to leave home and trusted him with the money. Without even listening to the son's confession or lecturing him on his behavior, the father received him with open arms and celebrated his return. In our own experience of the loneliness and alienation of sin, our motives for repentance may be quite mixed. But God takes care of that. His love is always there, freely offered as gift. No matter how often we turn away from it, he never withdraws it. We have only to reach out. When we experience his forgiveness, we understand all the more our sinfulness, and we respond by trying to live as his children. Works of penance and atonement naturally follow.

God's prodigal love

Not a few in our Christian community fit more easily into the role of the elder brother, annoyed at the possibility that sinners get off so lightly. But the father has forgiveness and healing for this kind of sin too. The parable is often called the story of the 'prodigal son', but the central figure is really the father illustrating the absolute prodigality of God's love, poured out spontaneously and without measure. In a sense, the words spoken to the elder son are addressed to each one of us, in spite of our sins: 'All I have is yours'. God's love is not conditional on our being worthy of it. Unlike some parents, he does not say: 'I will love you if you behave properly'. His attitude is rather: 'If you accept my love, you will not want to sin.'

At this point, however, it is important to warn against trivializing sin and God's forgiveness. One can become almost sentimental picturing a grandfather God who overlooks our misdemeanors and loves us out of our badness into his own wonderful goodness. Sin is more than mere personal wrongdoing for which we can ask pardon and try to make amends. There is a deep mystery of evil in sin which is rooted in our human condition. Our human nature has dark forces and mysterious power within itself which are not simply the effects of social deprivation, of mental or physical disorder, but are rather stirred up and released by these. We are all sinners in the very depths of our being, and so we all need healing. There is so much we do not understand about the mystery of evil, and sin is essentially evil. Forgiveness on this level is more costly than we can appreciate. God, in Jesus, entered fully into our human family and took upon himself our burden of sin. He 'became sin' for our sakes. His very presence provoked and brought out the evil in men, to be soaked up and neutralized in his silent, suffering body as he went to the cross and accepted the criminal's death. This is the cost of our healing. There is a deep awareness of the mystery of sin behind the church's joyful song at the Easter vigil: 'O happy fault which gained for us so great a redeemer.'

Message of salvation

The first preaching of the apostles was that in Jesus, God had reconciled all men to himself, that in him we have the forgiveness of sin. This is salvation and liberation present in the church as a here and now reality, the firstfruits of the resurrection of Jesus, the beginning of new life in the Spirit.

People need to hear this message of salvation, but more important still, they need to experience it. The real test of the efficacy of any of the various forms of the sacrament of reconciliation is that it brings about real reconciliation and healing. In the ministry of Jesus, forgiveness and healing went hand in hand. In a certain sense, should we not ask: where is the healing that will prove that the church has the power to forgive sins? (Mt 9:5). If the church is to be a light to the world, it must be a credible witness to the love of God incarnate in Christ. It must give a continual example of mutual pardon, of fraternal love. If the church is truly catholic, it must be a home where all the members feel at home, a fellowship which overcomes the barriers and divisions of sin and selfishness. If the church is the sacrament of Christ, it must be the visible sign of his forgiving love. Not a sign pointing elsewhere, but an open invitation to a community in which men are healed and made whole, reconciled to each other, made friends with each other, and with God.

10

CAN MORALITY BE TAUGHT?

The new thinking on many of the topics touched on in the previous chapters has been a source of confusion and upset for large numbers of people since the Council. But what many serious-minded people, particuarly parents, teachers and pastors, are more immediately concerned about is what is sometimes called the 'break-down of morality'. They can accept the 'sinfulness' of the 'world', but they feel helpless when faced with the seeming rebellion of the younger generation of Christians. They find it hard to understand how children of good, church-going parents can so easily reject the moral standards they were taught at home, in school and in church. The immediate reaction of a father or mother to a teenage member of the family on drugs, having a baby before marriage, or going for an abortion, is to ask: how did it happen, why did it happen? So often they insist: but I *told* them it was wrong, they *know* they shouldn't behave like this. Sometimes the reaction becomes an agonizing self-recrimination: where did *we* go wrong, did we fail them in any way?

Is it so bad?

It has always been the mission of prophet and preacher to point to the sins of society, to alert people to the immorality of the times. We need such reminders. But the moralizing can be overdone. It has become almost a *cliche'* to speak of the permissiveness of today's world and complain about the church going to the dogs. It is natural too to look for scapegoats. Some bishops blame theologians for 'confusing the people' (as

though they were never confused by bishops), priests
blame parents for not exercising control in the home,
parents blame teachers and pastors for their failure
to give clear moral principles, and everybody blames
the 'world' or the 'media.'

Each group pointing a finger at a particular scape-
goat should realize that there are three other fingers
on the same hand pointing back at themselves. 'Passing the baby' is part of the psychology of sin described
in the Genesis story at the beginning of the bible.
Since each one of us is, whether we like it or not, 'our
brother's keeper', we all have a share in the responsibility. The failure may be unconscious, and therefore without sin, but our unwillingness to accept
responsibility or to do anything about it can indeed
be sinful. It is not the purpose of this chapter to point
a finger in any one direction, but rather to raise questions that will stimulate reflection. As in so many
other areas of Christian faith and living, perhaps
there are many things we have taken for granted in the
area of teaching morality that need to be looked at a
little more critically.

First and foremost, the facts must be seen in perspective, without panic. It is simply not true that the
world is in a worse state now than ever before. Only
people who know nothing of history speak like this.
We may feel that we are further off from heaven than
when we were children, but this is generally no more
than feeling. The myth of the golden age is as old as
human history; we all tend to look back nostalgically
on the past and see it through rose-tinted spectacles.
A generation or two ago perhaps there was less gang
violence or sexual promiscuity in our immediate
neighborhood, but it is a very large assumption to
claim that the overall moral climate was better. Social
conditions were different, sanctions were stronger,

and for many people the possibilities for wrongdoing were extremely limited. The old sailor with little material for confession after several years at sea could give as his excuse: plenty of temptation but little opportunity. For previous generations, even the temptations were limited. The fact is that the world has changed more in the past fifty years than in all of previously recorded history. Today's youngsters have to cope with pressures far more subtle and complicated than those known to their parents, and they are faced with a vast variety of choices that were simply undreamt of in the past.

Culture-gap

There is simply no way of comparing generations in any worthwhile way. The parent who begins his lecture: 'when I was your age', is liable to be told by his teenage son or daughter: 'but you were *never* my age'. James Michener's novel *The Drifters* is a graphic description of the vastness of the culture-gap between today's adults and their teenage offspring. It is no longer simply an age-gap or a generation-gap. It really is a culture-gap. Many aspects of the cultural shift are highlighted by Alvin Toffler's fascinating *Future Shock*, but philosophers and theologians claim that for the past few decades mankind has been undergoing one of the greatest cultural changes in its entire history. They describe it in terms of the shift from classical to historical consciousness. This change involves a whole new outlook on reality, and reaches into every area of experience. Vatican II adverted to it, for example, in the document on *The Church in the Modern World*: 'The accelerated pace of history is such that one can scarcely keep abreast of it...and so mankind substitutes a dynamic and more evolutionary concept of nature for a static one, and the result is an immense series of new problems, calling for a new endeavor of analysis and synthesis' (n.5).

Part of the problem in today's church is that people talk about morality and the teaching of morality with practically no reference to this change. But the change affects both our notion of 'morality' and how it can be 'taught'. It is taken for granted that there is a revealed and timeless morality that has only to be taught or handed on, but in fact there are question-marks over both the content of morality and the ways in which it can be taught. So many people look to the past or to some revelation from above as the source of moral teaching. But it is significant that even in the area of dogmatic truth, the Vatican Concil speaks of revelation as an ongoing process, continuing into the present. It says that 'Christ reveals man to himself' and gives meaning 'to the riddles of sorrow and death' (Church in the Modern World, n.22). 'Believers, no matter what their religion, have always recognized the voice and the revelation of God in the language of creatures' (ibid. n. 36). In his self-revelation 'God spoke according to the culture proper to each age' (ibid. n. 58). Speaking of revelation as a continuing process to be newly expressed for every age in prophetic witness, it says that 'it is the task of the whole people of God, particularly of its pastors and theologians, to listen to and distinguish the many voices of our times and to interpret them in the light of the divine Word, in order that the divine truth may be more deeply penetrated, better understood and more suitably presented' (ibid. n. 44).

Changing morality?

With regard to the 'content' of morality, enough has been said in previous chapters to make clear that no moral problem can be solved by a quotation from scripture or an ecclesiastical document. There is no 'package' of detailed moral truths to be simply preserved and handed on intact to later generations. The church's function is to remain faithful to the Spirit of Christ, to preach in word and deed the good news of salvation and the liberation we have in Jesus, and try to live out his commandment of love. But how the commandment of love is to be understood and implemented will depend on man's understanding of himself and of his world in each culture. There have been radical changes in the church's moral teaching through the centuries. There is no shortage of examples: with regard to slavery, property, usury, war, women, sexuality, marriage, responsible parenthood, organ transplants, social justice, church-state relations, conscience, conscientious objectors, freedom and human dignity, peace. It is a false loyalty to the church, and no loyalty to truth, to pretend that the changes were all minor modifications. Changes on all of these subjects were substantial, indeed radical.

Had people been aware of the provisional character of most of the church's statements on moral matters, they would be less upset and confused when faced with change. But if the statements themselves had been presented less dogmatically there would be less need for humility in admitting that they needed to be modified or perfected. The Vatican I statement that the Pope is infallible when teaching as head of the church on matters of faith or morals, is frequently quoted in support of a particular 'teaching of the church', but it is seldom recognized that the church has never made an infallible statement on a matter of morals. The point being made here is not that one can lightly dismiss the church's moral teaching because it is not infallible, but simply that people need to understand the changeability of morality. As already explained, this does not mean a morality without norms or a private conscience cut loose from objective standards. It simply emphasizes the cultural conditioning of all concrete norms, and the fact that answers from the past cannot solve new problems.

While we can rightly claim to have high moral teaching in the new testament, a knowledge of history should keep us from boasting too much. Only too often through the centuries the church imbibed and reflected the prevailing values of the times, and its record in the fight against colonialism, slavery, anti-semitism or racism is nothing to be proud of. Though we can make allowances for historical context, the church was no better than the secular state when it justified torture and the death penalty for heresy. Please God, we have come a long way since then.

Common search

When it comes to discovering solutions to new moral problems, the whole people of God, pope, bishops, theologians, priests and laity, simply have to work towards them with their God-given human reasoning power. The simple commandment 'Thou shalt not kill' will not solve the intricate problems of medical ethics, nor have we any formula of solution for the new questions arising from the population explosion, genetic engineering or brain-transplants. In this common search it should be stressed that in a sense the whole church is a learning church and the whole church is a teaching church. Married people have a lot to teach celibates about the experience of marriage, and priests and laity can learn from each other. Likewise, the church learns from its past, from its mistakes, from other Christians, who have their own experience of the Holy Spirit, and from the surrounding world.

Bishops and theologians have special teaching functions and they collaborate in promoting faith, and
both serve the church.

As part of their pastoral responsibility, the pope
and the bishops have a special authority in the area
of teaching, though they are by no means the only
teachers in the church. In carrying out this responsibility they have a grace of state available to them,
but it does not operate automatically. They have to
take the ordinary means of research, study, consultation and prayer to formulate their teaching. But they
have no access to sources beyond the reach of the body
of the faithful, nor are they empowered to produce
'new teaching', to tell the faithful things they would
not otherwise know. In the area of infallible pronouncements on matters of faith, pope or council can
only 'define infallibly' what is already the faith of the
church. In the question of categorical morality (i.e.
teaching in particular areas of morality), right and
wrong cannot simply be 'decreed' and 'accepted'. It can
only be preached and urged, backed up by persuasive
reasoning inspired by the gospel and the tradition
and experience of the church. In this area, the support
of the Holy Spirit does not guarantee the truth of the
teaching, but simply prevents the church from falling
finally and definitively into error.

Teachers of freedom?

When Jesus took leave of his disciples, he commis-
sioned them to 'Go to all peoples everywhere and make
them my disciples' (Mt 28:19). Thus, he entrusted
his teaching function to his church, to the whole community of his followers, to be shared in different
ways by all. There are bishops, theologians, scholars,
teachers, missionaries, counsellors and friends. But

the most important teachers for those born into a Christian community are their parents. It is from them that we get our faith and our understanding of morality. Their work is continued by teachers in school and by priests in church. Parents, teachers, priests, all have their part to play in the teaching of morality, and in a sense all are extensions of the teaching church embodied in the pope and bishops. But some questions arise about the teaching process today which may give food for thought to the various teachers in the chain.

Speaking of education, the Second Vatican Council affirms 'that children and young people have the right to be stimulated to make sound moral judgments based on a well-formed conscience and to put them into practice with a sense of personal commitment' (Christian Education, n. 1). It urges those responsible for educating others to try to form 'men who will be lovers of true freedom, who will form their own judgment in the light of truth', and it stresses that 'one of the key truths in Catholic teaching is that man's response to God by faith ought to be free' (Religious Freedom, nn. 8, 10). Paul frequently speaks of the 'glorious freedom of the children of God' (Rom 8:21). He urged the Galatians to 'Stand as free people, and do not allow yourselves to become slaves again' (5:1). He told the Corinthians that 'where the Spirit of the Lord is present, there is freedom' (2 Cor 3:17). Jesus himself promised his followers: 'If you obey my teaching, you will know the truth, and the truth will set you free' (Jn 8:31-32).

These quotations come from a variety of contexts and would need careful explanation, but there is no denying the emphasis on freedom. The salvation we have in Jesus means liberation from the slavery of sin and from the imprisonment of ignorance and fear. A basic concern of Christian formation, therefore, should be to enable people to grow as free persons, to encourage personal responsibility and moral maturity.

Inhibited growth

But our teaching has frequently been unsuccessful in this, and large numbers of people are imprisoned by an immature conscience, live in constant fear, and have seldom experienced true freedom. This is not the place to discuss the various methods of catechesis, but a point may be raised for those who hanker after the clarity and security of the old catechism and the black-and-white absoluteness of the moral rules that went with it. The traditional catechism was largely a condensation of the theology text-book, a summary of grown-up beliefs. It was taught to children to prepare them for life, as though they were simply adults in miniature. We looked for an adult response of faith from adolescents and young children, and in many cases we took it for granted that they had such faith because they had learned the answers to our questions.

In the area of morality, we did not make quite the same mistake, because we taught them rules reinforced by rewards and punishments, which is what they understood in those early years. In the same way as they learned behavior acceptable to the parents (toilet training, table manners, etc), they learned a list of 'sins' punishable by God in hell and good deeds rewarded by God in heaven. God was used as a cudgel to ensure that they would conform. Indeed he was sometimes used as a threat to have them conform to the social prejudices of the parents. Children were told that 'God would not like' certain things, although there was no way of knowing whether he had ever even expressed an opinion on them.

Many people outgrew the childish fear provoked by the 'God as threat' as they matured morally. But much of the church's practice continued to rely on this fear in getting people to 'behave', and many were thus kept at a childish level of response. In the area of dogma we treated even small children as adults in the material we taught them, while in the area of morality we continued to treat grown-ups as seven-year-olds. Missing Sunday Mass was declared to be a mortal sin, punishable by hell-fire, while for centuries we did nothing to make the eucharistic celebration a meaningful experience. For large numbers, it is still a matter of 'obligation'. Like any large society, the church needs law, but the multiplicity of laws attempting to provide for every foreseeable eventuality would seem to imply that people are not to be trusted to do the right thing in a given situation. It was forgotten that people only become trustworthy through the experience of being trusted.

Less than a hundred years ago Pope Leo XIII wrote to the archbishop of Paris: 'To the pastors alone is given the power of teaching, judging and ruling; the people must allow themselves to be governed, corrected and led to salvation.' In spite of the insights and ideals of Vatican II, this paternalistic attitude is not quite dead in the church. It is traditional Catholic teaching that parents must make decisions for their children, but they can be guilty of sinful neglect if they do not help the children to grow towards freedom and autonomous decision. This is particularly true in the area of morality. Is it not bordering on the sinful when church practice tries to guarantee morality by pressure and sanctions, apart from those cases where sanctions are absolutely necessary? So often there is an appeal to 'loyalty' and 'obedience' to accept a particular ruling instead of an effort to convince and persuade people's conscience. Authority is too frequently substituted for reason.

Challenge from youth

People who are accustomed to having most of their moral decisions already made for them, who have been trained to think of morality in terms of obedience to rules handed down, are ill-equipped to make conscientious judgments when they are suddenly told to 'follow their conscience'. This is the dilemma of many parents at the present time when they are challenged by their teenage children. They do their best to 'hand on' the moral truths they themselves received from home, school and church. They grew up in a society where conformity was rewarded and questions seldom allowed. But their children live in a different world.

The 'traditional teaching' can be passed on in terms of moral precepts, but it is much more important that children be taught the mechanics of moral evaluation and personal conscientious judgment. With methods appropriate to each stage of their psychological development they should be helped to see what factors need to be considered in any given situation, how they are to be balanced one against the other, and how one decides on what is morally the best thing to do. The answer cannot be given in advance. But once they leave childhood, nobody can make their decisions for them. It may be upsetting for parent, teacher or priest to see the youngsters decide on and do things we consider 'wrong' or 'sinful', but unless they have the freedom to make mistakes, whether or not they actually make them, they will not grow in moral maturity. God respects our freedom in the initial act of faith, and we must respect it in each other. The person who is prevented from ever making a mistake may also be prevented from ever growing up.

Sharing values

Parents, teachers and church leaders may hand on the moral wisdom of the church enshrined in commandments and rules, but the real problem is to communicate the values behind such norms. Information is not enough. Likewise, mere conformity, or obedience to an external law (thou shalt not steal, kill, etc), is not virtue. The virtuous action is the one done out of the conviction that it is the right thing to do. But it is too easily assumed that values (like truthfulness, sincerity, justice, etc) can be 'transmitted'. In fact, values are not personal values unless they are 'discovered' and personally chosen as worthwhile, as something worth striving for, paying for, making sacrifices for, as values one wants to live by. The challenge is to create an atmosphere and environment in which children and young people discover moral values as really valuable.

They will not be convinced by exhortations from parents or others to tell the truth, go to church, or be fair to others if they find those same authority figures continually telling 'white lies', being careless about church attendance themselves, or boasting to each other of 'good' business deals which patently involved unjust practice. Even small children are highly sensitive to such inconsistency, and what they follow is not what they are told verbally, but what they see 'done' and what they think 'works'. Parents sometimes complain of the 'materialism' and 'permissiveness' of the younger generation, but are quite unaware of how much these things are part of their own thinking and how much their practical judgments are influenced by them in spite of theoretical attachment to the principles they preach. Our own double-think in many areas of morality may be partly responsible for the moral confusion or rebellion of the younger generation.

Moral development

There is a vast amount of research by developmental psychologists from which valuable lessons can be learned by those concerned with moral formation. The lessons are not only for parents forming their children or teachers dealing with students, but also for Holy Mother Church helping the faithful towards the freedom of the children of God. Kohlberg and practically all the experts in this field have found a consistent positive relationship between conscience and parental punitiveness. Punitive aggression by the parent leads to aggression by the child, but it does not lead to moral learning. The old pattern of lecturing, rewarding and punishing may produce conformity, which may have the appearance of virtue, but does not lead to moral development.

Even the lecturing has its weaknesses. Parents often admonish their children for bad behavior with the complaint: 'You should know better!' In many cases, the youngsters *do* know, and the gap between knowing and doing is one we all experience, and even St. Paul admitted to it. But over and above this tension, which is simply one of the effects of original sin, there is the fact that so much of our moralizing is cerebral, limited to abstractions, and presented in words that are not meaningful to young children. An eight-year-old sees no connection between the principles he is taught about respecting other people's property and taking fruit from a vendor's basket. The reason why our efforts at moral training so often meet with disappointment is that they rely too much on the intellectual approach. Children are sometimes called 'little liars' at an age when the haven't the faintest idea of what a lie is in moral terms. They tell lies out of fear or as an enjoyable exercise of creative imagination, but they have no intention of deceiving anyone,

much less of harming. Adults who read moral meaning
into quite innocent events or insist on extracting
'confessions' under threat of punishment can be guilty
of mental cruelty to children. Such attitudes not only
do a great deal of psychological harm, but actually
stunt the moral growth of children.

Lack of love

There is considerable statistical evidence to show
that delinquents tend to come from homes where an
excessive amount of corporal punishment was ad-
ministered. When children who suffered in this way
are old enough, their reaction to the blind, unreasoned
way in which they were handled is expressed in anti-
social aggression. They have not learned respect for
authority and show no signs of a healthy conscience.
The excessive nature of the punishment and the inconsistency of its application leaves them feeling a
lack of love and of basic trust, thus depriving them
of two of the essentials on which mature moral living
depends.

Strange as it may seem, the children of toally permissive parents are deprived in precisely the same
essentials. The parents may give them money and
seemingly endless freedom, in fact everything except
what the children need most of all, namely the gift of
themselves and their genuine care. Such children may
boast to their peers that their parents do not care how
much they spend or where they go, but when they get
into trouble the boast sounds very hollow. Deep down,
they know that what they are really saying is that
their parents don't really 'care'. Of course, it may well
be that the parents *do* in fact care, but their neglect
or ignorance of what caring really means can prevent
the children from discovering and feeling their love.

It follows that some form of moderate punishment
can be an element in moral training. It can help in the

development of responsibility as young people learn to accept the consequences of their actions. Likewise, rules have their part to play insofar as children discover that even limitations on their freedom are for the sake of a greater freedom. But neither punishment nor rules will result in moral development unless the individual gradually discovers for himself that it is good to do the right thing.

This discovery is a slow process. In fact, developmental psychologists, as was mentioned in chapter 7, have discovered at least four clearly-defined stages of moral awareness that the young person passes through from childhood to late teens. Some adults progress a further stage or two, but many never even make it to the fourth and are still stuck on a lower level. How many grown-ups still have the childish attitude: 'If only God didn't exist, what a great time I could have!' Any efforts at moral formation must take account of the gradual nature of this development, with special emphasis on the word 'growth'. Moral formation is a lifelong process of growth, not merely in knowledge, but in sensitivity, imagination and feeling, a growth in wholeness.

Whole person

The moral response must be a response of the whole person, so the formation of conscience cannot ignore the emotional and affective aspects of life. Reasoning, will and emotions are all involved. Reason is essential. Knowing the good is not just a matter of being told what is right, but of understanding and being convinced that it is right. The efforts of all educators of conscience, therefore, should concentrate on raising the level of people's reasoning in moral matters rather than imprinting rules and regulations. Many parents are at a disadvantage insofar as their own experience was largely the acceptance of rules, so they cannot

be blamed when they feel helpless as they see their
rules and values questioned or rejected by today's
youth. It is not their fault that they were not encouraged to question or reason, that they were simply told
what was good for them. A one-sided preaching on
obedience, dependence and humility made them feel
guilty at the mere thought of questioning. They de-
serve a great deal of sympathy, but they need support
and help.

One of the greatest needs in the church at the present time is for adult education, with a program whose
content and methods would be geared for adults, not a
repeat of childhood learning. It is too easy an excuse
to claim that 'people are not ready for it', that the
'simple faithful' do not want to be disturbed. It can
be sinful neglect on the part of the church to continue
a policy that actually keeps people at a lower level of
moral development, that prevents them from giving
more of their intelligence to God.

Personal values

Raising the level of people's reasoning in moral judgment is one of the essentials of moral formation. But
since the reasoning will be not only about facts, but
also involve a response to values, people need a community and atmosphere which will enable them to
discover real values for themselves. They need a community at home, in school and in church in which they
discover for themselves how good it is to live by the
principles of justice, truth, sincerity, fidelity to promises, concern for the weak, respect for persons. It is
difficult for them to discover such values if they have
never experienced them in a meaningful way in their
own lives, or if these values are clouded or betrayed
by the institutions or standards of society. The real

values in our lives are the standards we live by, not the abstract ideals we verbally subscribe to.

Since the whole fabric of Christian living is simply the putting into practice of Christ's law of love, the basic value underlying all the others is love. Children and young people need to see that there is real love behind all the rules and regulations, that to search for solutions to moral problems is really to look for the best way to respect each other's rights, to love each other, and to enable each other to grow. The love in question is not conditional love, in which the parents love the child only insofar as it is an extension of themselves, reflecting their opinions and meeting their demands. It is genuine love, reflecting God's own love, in which the child is loved for its own sake, in spite of its faults.

This is the test for many parents today, when their teenagers experiment with drugs or sex, neglect or reject their religion, or become total drop-outs. A good practical definition of love is 'staying in relationship'. It calls for a great deal of selfless love and real concern to keep open the lines of communication with a son or daughter who seems to reject everything we stand for. But to reject them is to reject the future generation of the church. To close our hearts against them is to teach them that the church is simply a club for nice people, not the community of the followers of Jesus in which forgiveness and reconciliation can be experienced as a gift from God. Prayerful reflection on the figure of the father in the parable of the lost son (Lk 14:11-32) may remind us of the Christian ideal in this kind of situation

Maturity the goal

The purpose of this chapter was not to outline a program of moral formation, nor to criticize the methods of the past, but to draw attention to the need for a critical look at the simple phrase 'teaching morality'. It is understandable that those in authority, parents, teachers, priests and bishops, should feel responsible for those in their care, feel the impulse to guard and protect them, and worry when they seem to drift away or show signs of becoming independent. They also feel responsible for the institution they represent, family, church, society, and they naturally tend to conserve and protect the wisdom and traditions of such institutions. A static society tends to have a static Christianity. But in both cases there should be less concern about conservative protection and more emphasis on growth. If they have the emphasis in the wrong place they can too easily become preoccupied with *control* rather than moral *influence*, and imagine that they have no *authority* unless they have *power*, hence the recourse to threats and sanctions.

The differences are important and far-reaching in their consequences. Preoccupation with power and control leads to a negative, condemnatory attitude to new ideas, and intolerance of pluralism, a deadening uniformity, an oppressive centralization, and no consultation in decision-making, all of which militate against the personal growth of individuals. Too much control can stifle initiative, and power easily provokes fear. The challenge to all teachers of morality is to release the God-given potential that is in each person, to create the encouraging, supportive community in which every individual is helped to grow towards ever greater self-autonomy and self-esteem. When Paul speaks of the variety of gifts in the church, 'apostles, prophets, pastors, teachers', he stresses that they are for the building up of the body of Christ, to enable all of us to 'become mature people, reaching to the very height of Christ's full stature' (Eph 4:13).

11

LET'S REHABILITATE SIN!

It would be a total misreading of this book to conclude that recent developments in scripture studies
or theology have done away with the notion of sin or
in any way minimized its importance. Nor can it be
said that they have so altered its description as to
empty it of meaning. On the contrary, running through
all of the preceding chapters is an implicit plea for a
rehabilitation of the word 'sin'. It has fallen on hard
times, and it needs to be rescued. In the world at large
it is an empty word, generally avoided, or used in the
most superficial sense. In the churches it has become
so trivialized that it touches only the surface of men's
minds, no longer finds an echo in their hearts, and fails
to help people change their lives. There is no need to
find a substitute word to sound more modern, because
it is one of the basic words of our religious tradition, a
word as fundamental as 'grace' or 'God'. In order to
rehabilitate it, we need to rescue it from the over-
simplification that keep people from taking it as
seriously as it deserves.

Neither symptom nor crime

To emphasize sin is to re-affirm moral responsibility,
to do people the honor of respecting their personhood.
Society's superficial reaction, as Menninger points
out, is to reduce sin to symptom or crime, so that all
that is needed is to treat the neurotics and punish the
criminals, leaving the rest of us with an easy conscience. But this is very much an over-simplification.
In the chapters on guilt and punishment we drew

attention to the need to recognize real guilt in whatever degree it is found, and to help people accept the consequences of their actions, which is the element of punishment. God does not inflict punishment, and we might do well to follow his example by seeing to it that penalties, either in civil society or in church community, are therapeutic, working for the offender's improvement, or in extreme cases affecting the common good, simply a deterrent. But vindictive punishment is simply collective revengé, and should have no place in Christian thinking.

To have dealt with the neurotics and criminals is not to have finished with sin. The big sin is to refuse to accept that we are our brother's keeper, to close our eyes to the fact that we are part of the system which encourages people to behave neurotically or criminally. So many of these are more sinned against than sinning. To draw attention to their unsocial or anti-social behavior is to distract from our own responsibility, to forget that many of our own attitudes and actions are far more harmful to society.

Recognize sins

We are continually sinning, but we prefer not to think about it, and the fact that so many people are in the same boat makes the evasion all the easier. The fact that dishonesty, pilfering, malingering are so common, means that the honest man is made to look eccentric. For the health of society, Menninger pleads for a new awareness of the seven capital or deadly sins, plus a few more: pride, greed, covetousness, lust, envy, gluttony, anger, sloth, waste, cheating, stealing, lying, cruelty. These are not simply diseases for which we are not responsible, pathological conditions we can do nothing about. There is no need to catalog the harmful results to society of any or all of these, nor to describe the basic unhappiness and lack of wholeness they bring to the sinner. But it would be a good thing to remind ourselves that they are bad, that we need to be converted from them and try to avoid them.

Society at large needs such a reminder, and the churches too need to have their conscience stirred. It is the function of preachers to keep the Christian community aware of the sins in our midst, to call us to repentance and atonement. But the purpose of this book was not to moralize about particular sins, nor indeed to enter into discussion as to whether different forms of contraception or sexual behavior are sinful or not. Rather it was to stir the conscience of Christians to reflect on the seriousness of sin, to re-think some of the assumptions and uncritical views that tend to trivialize it.

Trivializing notions

Thus, we saw how narrow and crippling is the influence of an over-simplified notion of moral law; a preoccupation with precise measurement; a disproportionate concern with sexuality, particularly physical actions, without reference to their full human meaning; judgment of isolated bits of behavior divorced from the overall pattern of moral living; an inflated and morbid super-ego taking the place of conscience; neurotic guilt feelings smothering the experience of real moral guilt; the punishment of sin seen in terms of an angry, vengeful God; the sacrament of reconciliation used mainly as a guilt-shedding process with little experience of real conversion; the notion of God's forgiveness as something to be worked for and earned rather than accepted and celebrated as healing gift; morality presented simply as rules

to be obeyed; unthinking conformity praised as obedience; the over-protective caution of those in authority, bishops, priests, teachers, parents; the failure
to raise the level of people's reasoning about moral
issues; the reluctance to promote autonomous moral
decision; the lust for clarity and certainty beyond
what is possible or appropriate.

To this list could be added more general factors like
concentration on private morality to the exclusion
of any awareness of responsibility for community
sinfulness like prejudice or discimination; a gigantic
blind spot with regard to sins of omission, and particularly the sin of simply not caring, not being concerned, and of not being concerned at our lack of
concern; an artificial separation between church and
world, spirit and matter, soul and body, worship and
service, love of God and love of neighbor, future life
and life here on earth; a water-tight division between
teaching church and learning church; a failure to
realize that the church is not only an institution with
its structures and laws, but also a fellowship of
brothers and sisters in the Lord, a sacrament of Christ,
a herald of the kingdom of God, a servant of the world
God so loved; the refusal to read the 'signs of the times'
in the light of the gospel as an ongoing revelation of
God's will; a failure to recognize the presence of the
Holy Spirit in other Christian communities and to
admit that we might learn something from them; a
complacency that prevents us from realizing the
wealth of new insights in the documents of Vatican II
and from admitting how radical a change in thinking
they call for.

Call to change

This is not meant to be a list of sins, though it could
provide material for a fruitful examination of conscience. Failures in these areas may not only be sinful,

but they can narrow our concept of sin and indeed our understanding of Christian morality. To speak like this may be upsetting to some Catholics who claim that they do not wish to be disturbed in their faith. This reaction merely underlines once again the need for adult education in the church, how necessary it is to explain that our faith is in Jesus Christ, but that our understanding of it will be colored by the culture in which we live. To want a 'simple faith' in a world that is no longer simple is a failure to hear God's call in the complexities of daily living, an escape into a fantasy world in which even God can be fashioned in our own image and likeness.

The irony is that those who complain about 'innovations' and a 'new theology' undermining their simple certainties and relativizing their many absolutes appeal to the 'teaching of the church' and fail to realize that it is the church itself which is calling them to change, through the authority of an ecumenical council. The Council documents are the 'official teaching of the church', more 'official' than any catechism produced before or after the Council. That they represent, in many cases, a combination of different theologies and leave some questions without satisfactory solutions should warn us against false clarity and misleading simplicity.

Without going into detail on the more intricate moral problems, they have much to tell us that is relevant to morality. Their insights and approach throw new light on many of the topics discussed in the previous chapters. First of all, it is significant that the Council totally rejected the special document on *The Moral Order* drawn up by the preparatory commission, a document which reflected literally the legalistic and casuistic approach of the textbooks. Instead of a separate document, the Council spread its teaching on morality over many documents as the need arose.

This is not the place for an extensive treatment of
Vatican II moral teaching, but we need to recall its
new perspective and the radical departure from a
tradition that was at least a few centuries old. It
looked to the bible, dogma and the life of the church
as sources for renewing moral theology. Ignoring the
old 'blueprint' notion of natural law as God's plan,
it presents Christian life as a gift from Christ, a fruit
of the Spirit (The Church, n. 7). It stresses 'the dignity
and freedom of the sons of God, in whose hearts the
Holy Spirit dwells as in a temple, and whose law 'is
the new commandment to love as Christ loved us'
(ibid. n. 9). It uses the word 'law' more in Paul's sense
of a framework or principle of faith rather than as
precise and detailed code (e.g. Church in the Modern
World, nn. 22, 24, 28, 32, 38, 41, 42, 43, 48, 50, 51, 78, 89).

God's call in today's world

The relativization of external law is an immediate
consequence of the Council's teaching on conscience,
discussed in chapter 6 above. It emphasizes that conscience is not omniscient or infallible, and we are
reminded of the fact that it can be blunted by sin. But
there is a firm insistence throughout on individual
responsibility, and on the freedom of man's response
to God. Faith is conversion from sin and a turning to
God, not once but continually as we grow in personal
relationship with Father, Son and Holy Spirit. But
nowhere does the Council suggest that the gospel,
church teaching or even the presence of the Spirit give
us solutions in advance. Though the people of God
believe that they are led by the Spirit of the Lord, and
get inspiration from their faith, they still have to
'discern in the events, the needs, and the longings they
share with other men of our time, what may be genuine
signs of the presence or of the purpose of God' (ibid,

n. 11). God's call is to be heard in the here and now, in the bits and pieces of everyday life, and to be sought afresh as each new problem arises.

The world and earthly values are no longer looked upon as temptations and distractions from spiritual life, but are recognized as part of the basic goodness of creation. The moral challenge to man is not simply to keep the law in order to get to heaven, but to develop his full potential, to grow into the likeness of Jesus, who is not only God made visible, but man made perfect. As Jesus did not drop out of the sky as an alien from another world, but was a man of his time who had to grow in age, wisdom and strength, so too the Christian is rooted in this earth, belongs to the human family and is part of its culture.

With this kind of vision, the Council resolutely rules out any kind of individualistic or otherworldly morality and piety. The document on *The Church in the Modern World*, whose opening sentence speaks of joy and hope (*Gaudium et Spes*), emphasizes human solidarity, cemented by love extending even to enemies (*ibid*, n. 28), and lists the principles or basic truths that should guide moral decisions: interdependence, co-responsibility and participation, respect for human rights and social justice (*ibid*, nn. 25, 31, 24, 29). It lays particular stress on the rightful autonomy of earthly affairs (*ibid*. n. 36).

Values before rules

The second half of this document is a treatise on values that ought to be a source-book for Christian thinking on morality, dealing as it does with family, cultural, economic, social and political values, and questions of international life, war and peace. This is a very far cry from the rule-morality and listing of sins

with their varying degrees of sinfulness so charac-
teristic of the old manuals, but it is now the 'official
teaching of the church'. In practice, therefore, the
church would not merely be faithful to its own teaching manifested in the principles of Vatican II, but also
be more effective as a teacher of morality if it were
simply to drop all attempts to draw a sharp line between mortal and venial sin, both objectively and subjectively. Concern about such a division has been a
mental strait-jacket of scrupulosity and fear for millions of Catholics, preventing their growth towards
moral maturity.

Likewise, the church in future will have much fewer
and far less detailed moral rules than in the past, and
will focus more on fundamental principles of moral
reasoning, a deeper insight into human and Christian
values, and a heightened sense of personal responsibility among the faithful. This could be upsetting
for those pastors who fear that they may lose 'control'
of their flock and experience a diminution of 'power'
in their ministry, but it will be a big step forward
for the church when they can stop worrying about
'putting people straight' or 'making them good', and
instead concentrate on their primary function, which
is to preach the Good News of Jesus.

'Christian' morality?

With so much talk of the 'autonomy of earthly affairs'
and the recognition of 'human values', it could be
asked 'what is *Christian* morality?' or 'is there such
a thing?' This question has occupied moralists for
some years past, and there is growing consensus on
the view that, in terms of *content* or specific commands, there is no Christian morality distinct from
basic human morality. The ten commandments of the
old testament and the virtues preached in the new

testament are all simply moral demands of human nature, applicable to all human beings. The insights of the Council make clear that Christians and humanists have the same grounds for knowing the difference between right and wrong, and should therefore collaborate in seeking solutions to the world's problems. It was for this reason that Pope Paul could address his encyclical letter on fostering the development of peoples, *Populorum Progressio* (1967), which is certainly a document about morality, not only to Catholics, but to all men of good will.

Once again, this could be upsetting to those accustomed to thinking of the church as 'possessing the truth' to be handed out to others, but again they need to be reminded that the Vatican II documents are now the official teaching of the church. However, there *is* something different about Christian morality. Just as the religious faith of the people of God in old and new testaments saw the obligations of human morality in a new context, in the context of the covenant relationship with God and as a consequence of the new life in Christ, our faith today enables us to view the demands of being fully human as a response to the call of God.

Faith makes a difference

Our faith provides us with a new stimulus and motivation to act morally, puts before us the attractive, impressive and challenging model of Jesus in his humanity, and through his Holy Spirit gives us the power to cope with our sinfulness and respond to the call. Furthermore, the teaching and example of Christ may make us more sensitive to ideals above the normal, like turning the other cheek, going the extra mile, foregoing our rights, loving our enemies, and remind us of a theology of suffering, of failure and the cross. Likewise, our belonging to a Christian community, a community of faith, service and worship can make demands on us like participation in the eucharist and celebration of sacraments that are not operative for non-believers. Also, our belief in a personal relationship with God leaves us open to the possibility of experiencing a special invitation from him not merely to continual conversion and greater intimacy, but also to a special way of service in the community, for example in the priesthood or religious life. Finally, belief in a God of infinite love, caring for us personally, can bring healing, growth and wholeness that will color our attitude towards our neighbors and the world about us. Faith also makes a difference in the understanding of sin. It considers sin not simply as selfishness, letting oneself down, disappointing or hurting others or breaking a law. Sin is all of these, but for the believer it is much more. It is the refusal to behave like a child of God, a failure to reflect the mind and heart of Jesus our model.

Man fully alive

These are all important differences, but they should not allow us to forget that underlying them all is the basic moral demand to become actually what we are potentially, to become fully human. If we are called to follow Jesus, who is not only God in human form but also the perfection of humanity, the more Christlike we become, the more fully human we become. There are individuals for whom the external expression of their growth in Christ will be blocked by obstacles beyond their control, so we must beware of a too-easy identification of holiness and psychological wholeness. There are forms and degrees of holiness known only to God. But the normal pattern is that our growth in Christ is a development of our humanity.

St. Irenaeus describes this ideal in his claim that 'the glory of God is man fully alive.'

But nobody grows alone. Our roots are in the earth, whose stewardship God put into our hands, and our life, health and growth are determined by our relationship with those around us. We are what our relationships enable us to be. To respond to God's call to grow, to be fully human, therefore, is to be in a correct relationship with these realities. In fact, we have no way of knowing whether we love God, whether our prayers are more than words, apart from the test of service, of love of our fellowman as Jesus himself tells us: 'unless you did it to one of these my least brethren'. Certainly, we need to pray and worship. Like Jesus himself, we need to be alone with our heavenly Father from time to time and we also need to praise and thank him together as a community. But, without the touchstone of service, we cannot be sure that this is not mere escapism, that our contemplation is not simply talking to ourselves about ourselves. There can be no love of God except through the neighbor. When Jesus calls us to serve God rather than the mammon of wealth, power or reputation, he is really telling us to live for others. But since we are to love them as we love ourselves, a certain healthy self-love and self-esteem is essential to being human and being Christian. This strand of our Christian vocation needs to be more openly acknowledged against a one-sided preaching on self-abasement.

Reality of sin

It would be easy to get carried away by the optimism of the positive picture of man's dignity and call as presented in the Vatican II documents. But a too-optimistic picture is bound to be shallow. The full picture must include the dark side of our nature, equally emphasized by the Council, namely the evil in our depths that can turn self into God, the pride, avarice, lust and aggression that are the effects of serving that false god. Our exaggerated self-love is a disorientation at the very center of our being. It is what we call sin, and it expresses itself in all kinds of broken, distorted and destructive relationships with those around us and with the material world in which we live.

The purpose of this book was to focus attention on the seriousness of sin, to rescue the notion from the many elements in our tradition that tend to trivialize it, and to remove the misunderstandings that tempt people to dismiss it as a reality. We need to see it not simply as misdemeanor, law-breaking, or surface action for which we can easily make amends, but as a mysterious, ever-present reality in the church as a whole and in individual members. It is a reality to be concerned about, but not to be unduly afraid of. 'Where sin increased, God's grace increased much more' (Rom 5:20). In Christ Jesus we have the forgiveness of all sin, but unless we are convinced of our sinfulness in all its depth and complexity, how can we realize how much we need him, or fully rejoice in the pardon, healing and new life he brings us?

Kathy Hardin
City of Hope Hospital
1500 East Duarte Rd.
Duarte, California
Hillquist Pavilion
Neurology Dept.